Caught by Grace

The Endless Possibilities When You Encounter Jesus

Alex Basile

ST PAULS

Library of Congress Cataloging-in-Publication Data

Basile, Alex.
Caught by grace: the endless possibilities when you encounter Jesus / Alex Basile.
    pages cm
ISBN 978-0-8189-1363-1
    1. Grace (Theology) 2. Jesus Christ–Friends and associates. I. Title.
    BT761.3.B37 2013
    248.4–dc23

                                    2013026405

Produced and designed in the United States of America by the
Fathers and Brothers of the Society of St. Paul,
2187 Victory Boulevard, Staten Island, New York 10314-6603
as part of their communications apostolate.

ISBN 13: 978-0-8189-1363-1

Printing Information:

Current Printing - first digit   1   2   3   4   5   6   7   8   9   1 0

Year of Current Printing - first year shown

2013   2014   2015   2016   2017   2018   2019   2020   2021   2022

CAUGHT BY GRACE

Visit our web site at
www.stpauls.us

or call 1-800-343-2522
and request current catalog

I dedicate this book to my children
Alex and Maggie.

Special Thanks to Jeff Harris for designing the cover.

Thanks to Tom Huggard for assisting with editing.

To Father Thomas Cardone for his spiritual
leadership and friendship.

To my beautiful wife Allison for the gift of her
love and inspiration.

TABLE OF CONTENTS

PREFACE

We all read and reflect on the Scriptures. Being nourished by the Word of God is part of our daily spiritual tradition. To know Jesus professionally (what he said and did) and personally (through prayer, meditation and reflection) is the goal of every believer.

Now Alex Basile shares his knowledge and personal relationship with Jesus by sharing those graces that he has caught along his spiritual journey through his daily diet of scriptural meditation.

Alex thrives when he is around his family, his friends, his colleagues and his students. Is this not what Christian communion and community is all about? To be alive personally and spiritually with others! We are best when we are with one another in the body of Christ.

In *Caught by Grace*, Alex shows us through Jesus how the Body of Christ was built; namely, by one encounter after another. The earliest friends of Jesus were caught by grace. Here they learned who they were and who they were not by being in the presence of the Son of God. Their experience of encounter enabled them to grow in relationship, which became the foundation of a new personal awareness of faith through communion.

Alex makes it very clear that we all learn and are challenged by the encounters that our biblical ancestors had with Jesus. Just look at the following encounters:

Peter and Jesus

John, the beloved and Jesus

A thief and Jesus

A bystander and Jesus

A sister and Jesus

No matter whom Jesus meets along the way, there is a lesson from the past; but more so there is a lesson for each one of us today.

Alex wrote *Caught by Grace* in 2012-2013, the "Year of Faith" which was proclaimed by Pope Benedict XVI. In this time of renewed and new evangelization, Alex invites us to place ourselves in the midst of these encounters of yesterday and make them come alive for ourselves as we struggle with living the gospel life of today. The graces of the past are still bestowed in this present moment. The trials of the past and the sins and vices, which were so predominant then, are still with us today. Think about the early disciples; we are very much like them today. As they were touched by grace; so are we. As they began to see God differently; so do we. As they saw endless possibilities by being in relationship with Jesus; so do we.

Immerse yourselves in the vision and inspiration of Alex Basile and allow his experience, his lessons and his faith to touch you. May you be caught by grace!

Father Thomas A. Cardone, S.M.

INTRODUCTION

When God created humanity, He bestowed the gifts of intellect and free will upon us. We have been given the ability to think, to reason and make decisions. He fashioned us so that we may love Him and love others. But there is a major roadblock that stands between us and a successful relationship with God: selfishness. Our will skews our ability to say and do what God desires. Because of our weakness and our tendency toward sin, God the Father sent His Son to guide us. Not only did Jesus spend countless hours teaching His flock the secrets of life, He also gave us the greatest gift, His grace. The only way to save His sheep was to lay down His life for them. The grace of Christ flows from His abundant self-giving love. It begins with the Incarnation and reaches its ultimate peak in the Crucifixion.

God clearly understands our afflictions. Our flaws are an opportunity to display His perfection through His grace. As the Lord spoke to St. Paul, He reminded us about His power:

> My grace is sufficient for you for power is made perfect
> in weakness.   *(2 Corinthians 12:9)*

Throughout the Gospels, we witness it repeatedly. Our corruption becomes His goodness; our sadness becomes His joy; our perversion becomes His perfection. No matter how deep the ditch may be, the hand of grace can pull us from its depths.

We watched the many people who encountered Jesus throughout His ministry as He journeyed to the summit of love, Mount Calvary. Many lives were transformed by the compassion and message of our Savior. We need to place ourselves in their shoes to see life from their viewpoint. What made them change? What did Jesus do or say to initiate conversion? How can we learn from them? These were real people who recognized the truth in Jesus. The lifestyle He offered was irresistible. They had become masters of confusion, virtuosos of doubt and despair lost in darkness and personal sin. Suddenly, light streamed into their lives from above!

Most of the people who met Jesus did not know that He would enter their lives. They trudged through everyday existence and had no idea how miserable they were without Him. After their encounter with the Teacher, suddenly everything changed. He offered hope. He showed that a relationship with God was closer than they thought. But Jesus also challenged them. He urged people to live according to a new standard. The commandment of love should rule their lives. Every decision must revolve around the question, "Am I doing what I can for others?"

Jesus redefined common terms such as "love" and "compassion." His grace brought heaven to earth. God now worked within us. The notion of God changed totally. He was not the vengeful tyrant who ruled with fire and brimstone. No longer was he judging us from the distance. He was a loving parent and brother who stood beside us every moment of our lives. A relationship with our heavenly Father is deeply connected to our other relationships. Before Jesus, people failed to see the God of relationship. Now people were aware that God's desire to love us meant that He, too, had to make difficult choices. The idea of the covenant with God was transformed with a sacrifice that went well beyond a cow or a bird. This new covenant required that the blood of His Son be shed for His creation.

Even with the gift of His life and His teachings, many people choose to reject what Christ offers. They would rather drink from the well that the secular world provides, even though it leaves them thirsty. Jesus offers an alternative. He is the salesman who is willing to give his product away. The gift that Jesus hands us is grace. Grace conquers sin and points us to salvation. Jesus entered into the world to physically and spiritually escort His creation to eternal life. The vehicle that carries us home is grace. This reward provides what we cannot do on our own. Grace becomes the constant leaning that pushes us towards the inclination of goodness and purity.

Throughout His ministry, Jesus told parables about God's forgiveness. He set aside all conditions for reconciliation. Because He made us, the Creator loves all of us the same. This profound love is infinite. The well never stops flowing. In the story of the workers in the vineyard, some workers do not arrive in the field until later in the day. When the owner pays his employees, everyone is given an equal reward. We may question the motives of the owner until we recognize that even the least of us may be the recipient of His amazing grace.

God's grace seems to have the most effect on those who are furthest from the Kingdom. Jesus opens the gates of heaven to anyone who will accept His invitation. Humans must first overcome the obstacle of selfishness. Grace assists us in this process. St. Francis reinforced this concept when he said:

Above all the grace and the gifts that Christ gives to us
His beloved is that of overcoming self.

Because of their inability to shed the layers of ego and narcis-
sism, the people that we will encounter in this book found it difficult to discover fulfillment. Many of the characters we meet never
anticipated the saving action of Jesus. They had given up hope. The
limited nature of their humanity had left them longing for more
and searching for someone to help them put the pieces back together. They soon discovered the benevolence of God as described
by literary giant Eugene O'Neill:

Man is born broken. He lives by mending. The grace of
God is glue.

As we fall apart, a relationship with Christ makes us whole
again. Grace is the magnet that draws us closer to Him. Once we
include God in our lives, anything is possible. Man may be the
burden upon himself, but God lifts the heaviness so that we can
rise to new life.

Look closely at the friends of Jesus in the chapters that follow and witness how grace remolded the deformed lives of sinners.
He transformed broken marble into another masterpiece. Christ
healed the spiritually sick and brought those who stumbled to their
feet. We often hear commercials promoting the gift that keeps on
giving. For the Christian, that gift is grace. It is presented to those
who deserve it least. Look closely at the lost and wretched souls
who discovered a new path to follow. Learn from His love and actions. Allow grace to reverse all that is wrong in your world.

CAUGHT BY GRACE

CHAPTER ONE

THE SINKING ROCK

After arresting him they led him away and took him into the house of the high priest; Peter was following at a distance. They lit a fire in the middle of the courtyard and sat around it, and Peter sat down with them. When a maid saw him seated in the light, she looked intently at him and said, "This man too was with him." But he denied it saying, "Woman, I do not know him." A short while later someone else saw him and said, "You too are one of them"; but Peter answered, "My friend, I am not." About an hour later, still another insisted, "Assuredly, this man too was with him, for he also is a Galilean." But Peter said, "My friend, I do not know what you are talking about." Just as he was saying this, the cock crowed, and the Lord turned and looked at Peter and Peter remembered the word of the Lord, how he had said to him, "Before the cock crows today, you will deny me three times."

(Luke 22:54-61)

Peter sat motionless in the darkness. His mind wandered back to the days on the Sea of Galilee. He imagined his long hair blowing in the wind, his face bronzed from working in the summer sun. His life was difficult, but required more brawn than thought.

Peter could command any crew, but he was powerless over the fish of the sea. His occupation did have its risks. The sea would be tranquil one minute and unforgiving the next. It was the only thing he knew before the Teacher came onto his boat and offered him the invitation he could not refuse.

Jesus had recognized Peter's ability as a leader. Most people referred to him as "Simon." The Rabbi gave the fisherman a new name. He would call him "Peter" or the "Rock." The Galilean would be part of the foundation of His new Church. Over the course of the few years that they had known each other, they had become the closest of friends. Peter witnessed the most important events of Jesus' ministry. Now as his friend had predicted, his cowardice would lead to denial.

After they had arrested Jesus, Peter stood by the fire hoping to sort things out. But as he warmed himself in the chilly air, he stared into the flames. Suddenly, they began gesturing toward him. The Gospel of Luke referred to the woman who questioned Peter as a "maid," but I have always imagined her to be an old shrew. Her fingers, shriveled with age, accusingly pointing at the first pope. We all know the type: more concerned with pointing out the flaws in others than recognizing the misery that brewed within her own heart. She squawked in her weakened voice, "This man, too, was with him." Peter looking to remove himself from the situation quickly rejected her accusation. But there were more people who knew Peter. He could not escape his near celebrity status. Everywhere Peter turned he was reminded of the good friend he had just allowed to be pushed into the uncertainty of the night.

The news had spread quickly around the city of Jesus' arrest. People wondered who would be next. After Peter denied Jesus a third time, we are told he went out and "wept bitterly" (Luke 22:62). Inconsolable, he did not know which way to turn. He desperately searched for an answer.

Jesus had plucked Peter from obscurity and brought him on the adventure of a lifetime. Peter must have often questioned what life would have been like if Jesus had never found him on the shore that day. His little boat seemed so far from the danger, but it was also far away from the joy that a life with Jesus provided. He taught Peter so much in the short time they spent together. Life now had endless possibilities, even beyond this present existence.

Jesus appointed Peter CEO of his new corporation, but he treated his Master like an employee scorned by his boss. Jesus gave Simon everything including the keys to the Kingdom and how did he repay Him? Contemplating the generosity of Christ made the tears flow even more. We seem to hurt the ones we love the most. We take them for granted and abandon them when our love is truly required.

This broken man teaches us many lessons about humanity. He inspires us to rise above the depths of despair. No matter how terrible things may seem, a relationship with Jesus provides the strength to overcome the most desperate of times. We know that Peter triumphed over this momentary darkness.

It was far easier to walk away from Jesus on that cold night before Jesus was crucified than it was to encounter Him after the Resurrection. Peter now had to face his master in the unwavering light.

Peter sought comfort by returning to the sea. Maybe a morning on the water would help bring some solace to his chaotic world. But like so many other days, the time on the water yielded nothing.

After a stranger had urged the apostle to return to deeper water, their luck changed. Peter had been convinced once before to make a second expedition onto the lake. This request made him and the other apostles realize that someone with incredible power was in their midst.

The risen Christ questioned the loyalty of His dear friend when they were reunited at the Sea of Tiberias. After breakfast, Jesus set the fisherman straight. Peter's new responsibility demanded that things must change. Many children hear the same words from a parent: "If you love me, prove it!" On the sandy shores of the lake he knew so well, Peter realized that there was no turning back. Love is a powerful word but only when reinforced with action. There would be plenty of time for eloquence. True discipleship meant sacrifice. The next time he tested his net he would not be collecting fish, he would be gathering the sheep for his flock. By the end of his life, Peter willingly demonstrated what it was to be Christ-like. When the speeches were finished, it was time to embrace the same cross that his friend embraced. In Rome, Peter was captured by Nero and crucified for his allegiance to the Savior. His conversion was complete.

Being associated with Jesus is not enough. Our Savior is saddened by the moments when we deny that we know Him through our actions and our words. We avoid the tag "Jesus freak" at all cost. In our effort to seem "normal" we prefer the dysfunctional to perfection. He hears our conversations and waits for us to stand up for Him. He watches as we retreat into the darkness looking to protect ourselves. Others question our association to Him, but we downplay it in order to fit into the crowd.

Jesus calls every Christian to lead others to Him in a world that does not necessarily accept what He taught. As Blessed William Joseph Chaminade stated, "We are all missionaries." Jesus urges us to steer the ship through the storm. We must be the rock for those at work, in our school, in our friendships and in our families. Others can use our faith and steadfastness to build their own relationship with God. Even in the most turbulent times, people will witness our need for God.

Jesus utilized Peter to illustrate how ordinary people become extraordinary Christians through self-sacrifice and love. We see what happened when the first pope acted selfishly without any regard for the will of God. Things began to unravel quickly. When our lives are focused on Christ, we, too, will be capable of incredible things. Assume the role of leadership to make Jesus a reality to others. When your faith in Jesus starts to waver, remember there is no comfort in the darkness.

Being a Christian requires us to leave the cover of our complacency. Following Jesus demands that we make some life altering decisions. As the fisherman moved from Galilee to Rome, his path was a mystery. Like Peter, we may not always know where we are headed, but one thing is certain: every step can lead us to a life of fulfillment and joy. When we plan our days, we fill our calendar with things we love to do. We have little tolerance for the challenging and unpleasant tasks that arise from time to time.

Our relationship with Jesus demands that we do leave the shelter of the harbor and venture into open waters. When the swells become too much to handle, Jesus is there to calm the seas. The story of Peter demonstrates how Jesus never sends us on a mission that we can't handle. He knows our talents and our strengths. Our leadership is needed. Come forward and be the rock for others and allow them to build a relationship with Christ on the foundations of your words and deeds.

Graceful Contemplation

1. Reflect on both moments of confidence and faith in your relationship with Jesus and times of yielding and becoming a sinking rock of cowardice and failure.

2. "We seem to hurt the ones we love most." Have you?

3. "True discipleship means sacrifice." Choices based on complacency, comfort and convenience suffocate a Christian's vocation while the road of self-sacrifice leads to life. Reflect on these personal patterns.

4. Christianity is missionary. Reflect on those who have brought you to Jesus and those who have looked to you for bringing them to deeper faith.

CHAPTER TWO

THE GREATEST DISCIPLE

Standing by the cross of Jesus were his mother and his mother's sister, Mary the wife of Clopas, and Mary of Magdala. When Jesus saw his mother and the disciple there whom he loved, he said to his mother, "Woman, behold, your son." Then he said to the disciple, "Behold, your mother." And from that hour the disciple took her into his home. *(John 19:25-27)*

When I was eight, my cousin Marianne was diagnosed with cancer. Doctors quickly realized that the disease had spread beyond any cure. Seeking any distraction possible, my aunt and uncle brought their family often to our house on Long Island. The support of family and the change of scenery provided a well-needed respite from the Bronx and a time to forget how illness was taking their daughter away from them.

As a father, I can't imagine how my aunt and uncle felt during that terrible year. The final days of this young life roared towards them like a locomotive without brakes. They would do anything to stop time, but it was useless. As the hands of time ticked by, all they could do was watch. No one understood this reality more than our Blessed Mother.

When the news reached Mary about the arrest of her Son, she probably took a deep breath and whispered, "The day has finally arrived." She had anticipated this horror since her meeting with the prophet Simeon in the Temple when Jesus was just a baby. She could never escape the old man's words, "A sword will pierce your heart." Whether she cleaned the house or cooked dinner for her family, the phrase may have haunted her. The sacrifice of her Son became the dark cloud that loomed on the horizon. She never knew when the storm would hit. Even though we try to focus on the positive, tragedy has a way of taking command of our lives. Mary was a realist. She had no delusions about the future. From the moment the angel came to her in a vision, Mary knew that her role as the Mother of God would be a challenge.

On Good Friday, Mary and the other women followed as the soldiers led Jesus to Golgotha. The other women must have thrown their arms around Mary to shield her from the blows of the hammer. As Jesus bled, so did her Immaculate Heart. She courageously took her place at the foot of the Cross. Her Son called from above and entrusted her care to the young apostle. Even at the point of death, the special relationship was evident between Mary and her Son.

When all was finished, they took Jesus down from the Cross. We have seen many versions of the Pietà. Mary embraced the body of her dead Son. She cradled Him in her arms as in Bethlehem. The body of the Savior seems almost weightless as Mary held the burdens of the world in her arms. She gazed longingly upon Him and perhaps yearned for another day with her family in Nazareth. But these thoughts would quickly dissipate because she knew that there is no room for selfish requests in God's plan of salvation. Mary's silence at the crucifixion exemplifies her complete surrender to the will of the Father.

At the Cross, Mary stood in contemplation and prayer. She focused not on herself but rather on her Son and the humanity He loved deeply. The many years in Nazareth prepared her for this day. She listened carefully when her Son spoke. She witnessed the commotion that He caused in the synagogue when He read from the prophet Isaiah and said, "This prophecy is fulfilled in me." Being a devout Jewish woman, she knew the Book of Isaiah well. As a mother, it was devastating knowing that her baby would become the suffering servant that the prophet spoke about. Seeing the brutality of the crowd Mary could easily have been bitter or angry. She had every right to wonder, "Why would He save them?" But she didn't. Instead, she probably meditated on the prophet's words:

> We had all gone astray like sheep, each following his own way; but the Lord laid upon him the guilt of us all. Though he was harshly treated, he submitted and opened not his mouth; like a lamb led to the slaughter or a sheep before the shearers, he was silent and opened not his mouth. *(Isaiah 53:7-8)*

Mary also demonstrates the importance of prayer. In her silent sorrow, she once again places herself in the hands of the Father. When life confronted Mary with questions she couldn't answer, she put herself in the presence of the Lord. Prayer might not provide us with every answer, but it allows us to reveal God's presence and peace. Consolation can never be found in constant questioning. As she prayed, she also listened for guidance from God. We also must speak to the Father with open hearts and minds.

Through the sacrifice of Jesus, Mary was transformed once again. At the crucifixion, Jesus gave her a new role as Mother of the Church and Help of all Christians. Her steadfast love and devotion make her the star that illuminates the darkness of disbelief. When the walls of life crumble around us, Mary's faith gives us real hope. Despair has no grip on a heart which has handed itself over to the will of God. We have a tendency to distance ourselves from our troubles and suffering. Mary's contemplation at the foot of the Cross illustrated her total communion with her Son's sacrifice. As an associate in the redemption of Christ, Mary gives herself at the crucifixion as well as Jesus.

Theologians refer to the self-emptying of Christ as "kenosis." It is through this process that He completely surrenders Himself to the will of the Father so that He can suffer and die for our sins. Mary endures her own kenosis at the crucifixion. There must have been very little left in the woman who stood bravely at the foot of the Cross besides her undying faith. The future Queen of Heaven exhibits the way to attain eternal happiness. It will not be what we take from this world, but what we freely give away.

The faith journey of Mary demonstrates the need for the ongoing conversion process throughout our lives. As in Mary's case, surrendering to the will of God may be only the beginning. Each chapter in our lives may require us to give even more of ourselves. How do you react to suffering and difficulty? Mary rose to every challenge. What will you do?

Many people buckle to suffering. I hear it often from my students, "My family stopped going to Mass when my grandma died." It is far easier to question what we do not understand rather than to submit willingly to the unknown. Tragedy can put a wedge between God and us. Instead of driving us away, suffering can forge us to Christ in a unique way. The Cross of Christ gives us strength to conquer anything that life may toss our way. Our Mother Mary shows us this.

The road did not end at the crucifixion for Mary. She remained with the apostles and was probably in their presence when they were told that Jesus had risen from the dead. Sorrow turned to joy in an instant. A relationship with Christ points to triumph even in times of despair. Mary teaches us that we must never lose hope. Death and sin do not have the final say in Christianity. Love does. Place yourself beside Mary at the Cross. Allow her strength to hold you up when you feel as if you are too weak to continue. Follow her example and encounter Jesus every moment of your life. When your heart is breaking, look up to Christ in adoration for He also understands your pain. In the moments when you can't see beyond the dark cloud that hovers above you, ask your Mother for guidance. Her faith and the light of her Son will overcome any storm.

Graceful Contemplation

Mary is not only the first disciple of Jesus, but also our intercessor as we say "Holy Mary Mother of God, pray for us sinners." In the Church, Mary has many titles: Our Lady of Sorrows; Our Lady of Perpetual Help; Mother of Good Counsel; Our Lady of the Rosary; Queen of Peace…

1. What dimension or spiritual quality of Mary serves as our help on the spiritual journey?

2. One author writes, "To live is to suffer; to survive is to find

meaning in suffering." What are/or have been your sufferings?

3. How do you face suffering?

4. Has your suffering hurt or helped your faith?

5. In times of trial, Mary trusts. This is easier said than done. Reflect on your ability to trust, both God and others.

6. In life, we often must deal with both hope and despair. Reflect on your ability to hope. Is love the last word?

CHAPTER THREE

THE UNINVITED GUEST

"Simon I have something to say to you." "Tell me teacher,"
he said. "Two people were in debt to a certain creditor;
one owed five hundred days wages and the other owed
fifty. Since they were unable to repay the debt, he forgave
it for both. Which of them will love him more?" Simon
said in reply, "The one, I suppose, whose larger debt was
forgiven." Jesus said to him, "You have judged rightly."
Then he turned toward the woman and said to Simon,
"Do you see this woman? When I entered your house
you did not get me water for my feet, but she has bathed
them with her tears and wiped them with her hair."

(Luke 7:40-47)

Y ou plan the party for months. You coordinate the menu, the
decorations, the music and the guest list. It begins to shape up
as the perfect gathering. Finally, the day arrives. Everything is in
place. You wait anxiously for your guests to arrive. As the doorbell
rings, you greet each guest with a welcoming hug. You make sure
that everyone has enough to eat and drink. As the party progresses,
you mingle and spend time with each guest. The conversation is
light and pleasant. No politics, no religion. Everyone seems to be
having a great time.

There is one guest that you had never met before tonight. A friend had decided to ask an acquaintance to tag along. This person would never have been included on your guest list. You do not know how they are going to act. You have no idea what they will say. Suddenly, people are uncomfortable. How do you get rid of the unwelcome guest?

Imagine how Simon the Pharisee felt after he had welcomed the popular rabbi into his house and she showed up! He watched with horror as she walked up to the guest of honor. "How dare she interrupt my party!" Simon peers around the room and ponders, "Who let her in? Who invited her?" Simon, disgusted by her mere presence, prays that she disappears. This woman is an embarrassment to this prestigious member of the Temple elite. "What if my friends see this hussy at my party?" Simon panicked silently.

Simon's stature in the religious community required him to adhere to certain standards of living. A woman such as this uninvited guest had no part in his life. If the other Jewish leaders learned of the events at this party, there would be certain consequences. Simon was scrutinized for inviting Jesus into his home. He heard the mumbling of the members of the Sanhedrin. They all wanted to know this young preacher from Nazareth, but Simon took the next step and invited Him into his home. In a quick instant, this woman of ill repute cast an ominous shadow over Simon's self-image.

Simon never seemed convinced that he should invite Jesus to his house. Jesus knew the truth. The actions of the woman puzzled the man. After the woman anointed the feet of Jesus with expensive perfume, she began to bathe His feet with her tears of shame. She proceeded by drying the feet of Jesus with her hair. We have all experienced when someone has invited us because of guilt, peer pressure or necessity. We sit at the party, feeling out of place. We are torn between hiding under the table and running out of the closest exit. Jesus must have experienced the "third wheel syndrome" as He felt out of place at this party. But being the Bearer of Truth, Jesus was not about to have the negative attention shift to this woman. Jesus knew her pain. He loved her willingness to admit her guilt. Not many people would throw themselves at the feet of another. That would be an act of shame. She didn't care what other people thought about her.

Instead, Jesus addressed Simon and questioned his intentions. The host, the master of the feast, was put on the spot. Simon, who had been anxious about the presence of this unexpected guest, now had bigger problems. The intended focus of the feast shifted now to the one who planned the party.

Jesus saw the disdain in their eyes. They hated the woman, not for what she had done, but for what she represented within them. We all have a tendency to do that. We see the errors of others and assume that we would never sin in the same way. It's much easier to see the faults of others, than to look within ourselves. Jesus did not hesitate to inform Simon that there was a huge difference between him and this woman. It was obvious to Jesus that Simon invited Him simply for the sake of having a celebrity in his midst. Simon apparently did not possess the qualities of a gracious host. Anyone can host a party, but not everyone practices the art of hospitality. Jesus had not felt welcome in the house of Simon until this woman entered.

Jesus took this opportunity to teach us about forgiveness. In His own life, Jesus had heard the words, "How could he do that?" many times. He understood that people hesitated to forgive because of anger, bitterness and resentment. He knew that these were obstacles to true communion with others. Many times our hesitation to forgive does not concern the severity of the infraction, but rather it reminds us of our own faults. At this event, Jesus was well aware of the self-righteousness of Simon and how this human tendency can be far more dangerous than the sins of the so-called sinful woman. It became easy for everyone at the party to isolate the woman and point at her with their guiltless fingers. Jesus turned the direction of their pointing inward and asked those in His presence to consider the importance of asking God for forgiveness.

Next time you begin to list the faults of another person, turn your attention back to yourself. Examine your motives and determine how your actions affect the people around you. Take this moment as an opportunity for change. Ask yourself the question, "How can I change to be a better person?" Use the misgivings of others to contemplate how you can serve God. Place yourself at the feet of our Lord and ask for His forgiveness.

Graceful Contemplation

1. There is a big difference between "my plans" or "Simon's plans" and "God's plans." Like Simon, we like to "control" yet God works through the unexpected. Do I allow myself to be surprised by God?

2. We often hear, "It's all about image"; yet spiritual authors, like Blessed William Joseph Chaminade remind us "that the interior is the essential." Where are my efforts – on the outside or the inside?

3. When an individual easily labels the faults of another, something is missing – genuine self-knowledge. When we understand and know our own shadow side, compassion towards others is the result. Is this my experience?

4. Christianity begins when we realize our sin and need for God – this is the Woman. When we fail to see our shadow side, our sin, our need for God is limited – this is Simon. Am I more like the Woman or am I more like Simon?

CHAPTER FOUR

THE POSER AND THE MISSED OPPORTUNITY

On hearing this Pilate asked if the man was a Galilean; and upon learning that he was under Herod's jurisdiction, he sent him to Herod who was in Jerusalem at that time. Herod was very glad to see Jesus; he had wanted to see him for a long time, for he had heard about him and had been hoping to see him perform some sign. He questioned him at length, but he gave him no answer. The chief priests and scribes, meanwhile, stood by accusing him harshly. Even Herod and his soldiers treated him contemptuously and mocked him, and after clothing him in resplendent garb, he sent him back to Pilate. Herod and Pilate became friends that very day, even though they had been enemies formerly. *(Luke 23:6-12)*

I had only owned the deli for a few months when the store was burglarized. The thieves ransacked the store, but only stole the loose change in the register and rolled coins that we stored under the counter. Anyone who has been victimized by robbers finds it hard to shake off the presence of the thieves in their home or their business. As I stood stunned behind the counter, I wondered how I would be able to conduct business without any coins to make change. Carl, the owner of a popular local restaurant, was one of the first customers of the day. When Carl heard of my predicament, he ran to his office and gathered all of the loose change he could find. Carl hoisted the coins onto the counter and gently whispered, "You can pay me back when you get on your feet." Without Carl's assistance, the first hours of business that day would have been utter chaos.

This began a long friendship with Carl. He and I sat for hours as he patiently explained his business philosophy. His restaurant ran like a well-tuned machine. His employees knew exactly what he expected from them. He was tough, but fair. His no-nonsense style earned him tremendous respect not only from his workers but from his customers as well. Carl included his son in his business empire. Carl Jr. became successful by riding on the coat tails of his father. The son lacked the grace and class of his father. His abrupt style alienated rather than invited. Everyone saw Carl Jr. for exactly what he was: a poor imitation of his father. Living in the shadows of your father is never easy. We often compare a son to his father, especially when they are in the same profession. This is what people did during the time of Jesus.

Herod the Great ruled Judea from around 46 B.C. until 4 A.D. Because this territory fell under Roman rule, the king was subject to their foreign influence. The Romans trusted and respected Herod's authority over his people. They knew the citizens of Judea feared this ruthless king. In a jealous rage, he killed his own wife. Herod murdered three of his sons who jealously eyed his throne. The Gospels explain that in order to prevent the arrival of a new king, he slaughtered every male infant in the vicinity of the "newborn king." The only benefit of Herod's rule was the prosperity and security that came to Judea. When Herod died, Caesar

Augustus split the kingdom between his sons Archelaus, Herod Antipas and Philip. Herod Antipas ruled Galilee.

Herod the Great and his son, Herod Antipas, both lacked any moral fiber. In no way would I propose that this king possessed any integrity whatsoever. But when the average person of Galilee came to know the son of Herod the Great, they quickly realized that Herod Antipas was merely a puppet. He ruled only a fraction of his father's kingdom. Herod the Great was certainly no role model, but people respected and feared him. The citizens knew that his sons lacked their father's strength. Nepotism gave them a powerful role in the Roman world.

The people of Galilee knew that Antipas was a poser, a person whose actions were motivated by how everyone felt about him. Herod Antipas heard the jeering and the open snickering. They would never dare say these things when his father ruled the land. Herod Antipas' biggest coup was stealing his brother's wife. But the real tragedy in the life of Herod Antipas was squandering the opportunity that his father never had, namely a chance to meet the King of Kings.

The Sanhedrin had sent Jesus to Pilate because the governor had the power to crucify him. The governor knew that he was thrust into a no-win situation. In an effort to rid himself of Jesus, Pilate sent him to his enemy, Herod, who was visiting Jerusalem. He was merely a guest in the territory his father had ruled. The king, delighted to meet Jesus, had heard of the Teacher and desired to see Jesus perform a miracle. Herod also saw this as a chance to win over the hearts of the Jewish religious leaders. Because of his selfishness, Herod missed a golden opportunity to change everything.

Unlike most Biblical episodes with Jesus, Herod does all the talking. He had waited forever to meet the Teacher. "So this is whom John the Baptist spoke of," he must have thought to himself. Instead of engaging Jesus in conversation, Herod grandstands in order to demonstrate to the Sanhedrin that he is truly important. The case against Jesus is weak at best, but he doesn't care. "This is my moment to shine," thinks the pompous king. "Father would be proud of me now," he could have rationalized. His father had used every circumstance, even moments like this to promote himself. This could have been the opportunity to turn it all around: the murder, the lust, the greed, and the cowardly ways. Herod could have wiped the slate clean. By stepping off his throne, he might have pleaded his case with the genuine King. "Master what can I do to inherit eternal life?" These words would instantly dissolve the years of hatred and self-indulgence. Herod forgoes the chance to fill an empty existence with something real.

Herod's experience with Jesus makes us realize that our consciousness of God does not suffice. A true relationship with Christ requires faith. The King of Kings stands before us so that we can learn from Him. When we fail to recognize His importance and use Jesus as a means of promoting ourselves, our interaction is meaningless. How often have we wasted a chance for true communion with Jesus? We often sit in church and think of the other things that we have to do. We look beyond Him as we chase after our narcissistic dreams.

Our time with Him at Mass becomes a burden rather than the pursuit of joy. We look to please ourselves rather than Him. Our presence is not enough. If we do not open our hearts to Christ, this time will be empty. Jesus presented Himself humbly before Herod.

He stood silently while the king shamefully exerted his earthly power. Jesus also makes Himself present to us so that we can change the direction of our lives. He points us to heaven. Will we choose to pursue our earthly goals and ignore Him as Herod chose?

Herod tried to impress everyone in his court, including Jesus. But the Savior knew Herod better than the king knew himself. Christ knew about Salome. He was conscious of the corruption. Yet, He allowed the tables to be turned for the time being. This was not the time to show His power and might. This king who was concerned more with the display of his own ego would never have appreciated any heavenly manifestation. Herod's unhealthy pride clearly overpowered his need for conversion. Herod starved himself spiritually only to fulfill his hunger with the sins of the flesh. Jesus also knows us. He knows what dwells deep within our hearts. Jesus waits for us to put aside our egos and go to Him. Will we do all the talking or will we sit and listen to the true Master?

Jesus promised that we would have many opportunities to come to His assistance. The hungry, the sick, the lost and the cold may not bear an exact resemblance to Him, but Jesus dwells in each one of these people. Will we willingly help the hurting or dismiss them after we realize that they do not satisfy our needs? Remove yourself from the kingdom of Herod; join a Kingdom that can change your world. Christ never hesitates to stand in front of us. Don't miss your chance to be with Him.

Graceful Contemplation

1. As Christians, we are called to live our vocations using faith
   and reason, yet sometimes these are set aside to favor only using

our emotions or feelings. Like Herod Antipas, we can act solely on emotions and make many mistakes. Reflect on episodes in your own life when you operated on feelings alone and did not think.

2. "Carpe diem" (Seize the Day). God presents endless opportunities in the journey of life. Reflect on both of these – opportunities seized and those missed.

3. Our first vocation is to be a good son or daughter, where we grow from total dependence, to independence, and finally toward interdependence. At times, this does not occur and we develop unhealthy psychological attitudes towards our parents like Herod. Has this been a personal pattern in your life?

CHAPTER FIVE

THE WALK UP THE HILL

Now one of the criminals hanging there reviled Jesus, saying, "Are you not the Messiah? Save yourself and us." The other, however, rebuking him, said in reply, "Have you no fear of God, for you are subject to the same condemnation? And indeed, we have been condemned justly, for the sentence we received corresponds to our crimes, but this man has done nothing criminal." Then he said, "Jesus, remember me when you come into your kingdom." He replied to him, "Amen, I say to you, today you will be with me in Paradise."   *(Luke 23:39-43)*

Jesus' curriculum focused on love and forgiveness. His parables revolved around God's desire to gather those who strayed from Him. People listened to His stories of the Prodigal Son and the Workers in the Vineyard and felt reassured that a relationship with God was still possible. Jesus must have heard their sighs of relief and seen their smiles ignited by His hope. He listened to them whisper to each other, "There's still time." God is the ultimate optimist. A cup of life is always half full. Even when we have completely lost sight of Him, He has faith that we will return. Even the most hopeless cases can be renewed by God's love.

One of the greatest conversion stories occurred on Good Friday. For the thieves that accompanied Jesus to Calvary, the crucifixion marked the culmination of a couple of miserable lives. Those who resort to crime may do so because circumstances provoke them to perform terrible acts. Criminal activity becomes a part of everyday living. Morality disappears. Their care and concern for others evaporates. His or her philosophy centers on personal gain at the expense of everyone else. We refer to these men as thieves but to receive the sentence of crucifixion they probably were guilty of murder as well.

Dragging the heavy cross through the cobblestone streets did not seem as bad as what awaited them on the hill ahead. The thieves had both witnessed crucifixions before. They were well aware that the Romans had made this form of torture a sport as well. An existence of deception and lies had finally caught up with them. They had eluded the grasp of Roman authority for many years, but today they would pay for their sins.

The thieves recognized the man who would join them on the path to death. He was not part of their criminal network. They had seen Him around Jerusalem. The crowds gravitated to Him. How could His followers turn against the preacher who seemed so benevolent and kind? They looked at Jesus and questioned how He possibly deserved such a fate as crucifixion.

Jesus' presence in the procession distracted the crowd's attention away from the thieves. Many displayed their disdain towards the Teacher. Many hurled insults at Him as if He disappointed them personally. But others wept as if their closest friend was being put to death. Why was there such a contrast in the way that the crowd saw this man? Perhaps no two people would be more appropriate to ponder this question than the contradictory figures of the two thieves.

The long walk to Golgotha did nothing to dispel the anger and resentment that had built up over the years. The piercing of nails only intensified the bitterness of the one man crucified next to Jesus. The other thief responded very differently to his situation and to the man crucified next to him. Instead of taunting Jesus, his words resembled a prayer. With all the strength he had, he pulled himself high enough on his cross to look Jesus in the eyes. He confronted the truth of his life. He pleaded his case and begged forgiveness. He reminded his angry counterpart that a chasm clearly existed between themselves and Jesus. "He does not belong here, but we deserve this," he said as he chastised his partner in crime.

We admire the good thief for his last-second conversion. His crucifixion was supposed to punish him for his sins. This could have been his last chance to spew expletives at the humanity that seemed to have forgotten him. Instead, he took the opportunity to make things right. He did not dwell on his imperfection; rather he focused on the man sacrificed for the sake of others. He may not have understood that Jesus had the power to pull him from the depths of sin.

Years of poor choices were instantly erased by the compassion of Jesus. The forgiveness of the good thief displays how salvation began immediately on Good Friday. From the moment that Jesus is placed on the Cross, humankind is saved from sin. The power of Christ's death can overcome a life of evil. A person simply needs to repent to benefit from the gift of His redemption. Jesus never hesitates to grant us forgiveness. We must initiate the process. Ultimately, the interaction with the good thief demonstrates that even through His pain and suffering, the Cross is as much about us as it is about Jesus. Our Lord does not focus on Himself, rather He thinks about how our sin destroys us. The Good Friday exchange pushes us to shut out resentment and hand ourselves over to Christ. We see firsthand how bitterness and anger will keep us from eternal union with Him.

For most of their lives the thieves fought the world without a relationship with God. This separation caused emptiness and despair to fester. The good thief came to the realization that he could no longer live without God. The sight of his counterpart on Good Friday clearly showed him that this choice made him miserable. Separation from God might not start intentionally. Many people drift from God gradually until they realize that something is missing or that life is falling apart.

Don't wait for a crisis to include God in your world. Examine your life and how you live. Ask Jesus today if you can become part of His Kingdom. Unite yourself with Him now. You don't have to wait until you look up the steep hill ahead to realize that He is absent from your world. Use the Cross as a symbol of love and forgiveness. Our insecurity and ego can keep us from a chance at eternal glory. The good thief waited until death stared him in the face until he contemplated a relationship with God. Discover peace in Christ today.

Being human, we constantly make a mess of life. We grab hold of our vices and refuse to let them go. Find consolation in the Cross. A second chance awaits each of us if we want it. When Jesus speaks to the good thief, He speaks to anyone who will listen. He summons every person to a life of holiness. We can attain this through our union with Jesus on the Cross. The realm of holiness awaits us. He not only remembers us in His Kingdom, but He anticipates our arrival at the gates. He has reserved a place for you. Show your desire to be part of it.

Graceful Contemplation

1. What is the cause of your resentment? Anger? Selfishness? Insecurity?

2. What keeps you from conversion and changing your life for the better?

3. What are the poor choices in your life that you regret? Did you have a pattern of poor choices? Did you have someone who was responsible for helping you move out of these patterns?

4. Christianity is about conversion and moving towards Jesus. Have there been a series of conversions that you experienced at various times in your life?

CHAPTER SIX

THE GREAT DEAL

After this he went out and saw a tax collector named
Levi sitting at the customs post. He said to him, "Follow
me." And leaving everything behind, he got up and followed him. Then Levi gave a great banquet for him in
his house, and a large crowd of tax collectors and others
were at table with them. The Pharisees and their scribes
complained to his disciples, saying, "Why do you eat and
drink with tax collectors and sinners?" Jesus said to them
in reply, "Those who are healthy do not need a physician,
but the sick do. I have not come to call the righteous to
repentance but sinners."   *(Luke 5:27-32)*

Bernard Madoff approached many friends and business associates with intriguing financial opportunities. People don't usually pass on the possibility of an easy buck. Madoff had a reputation of being a man with the "Midas touch." Everything seemed to
turn to gold around him. It didn't matter to people that his newest
venture seemed too good to be true. Even better. Greed has a way
of blinding us. When Madoff presented his alluring hedge fund,
people jumped at the opportunity to invest.

Many potential investors suspected that Bernard Madoff was

cheating. When they saw the large dividends that were being realized, they guessed that insider trading was the reason for the big
payoff. Moral law says that you avoid people and situations like this
at all cost. Instead, Madoff became a magnet. He attracted people as a light draws the moth from the darkness. Many search for
the secret to success. Madoff seemed to possess the golden ticket.
When investors looked for several billion dollars in redemptions,
the scam was revealed. Madoff's "Ponzi scheme" allegedly stole
more than fifty billion dollars from people who put their faith in
the business guru.

Since the genesis of humanity, we have judged the worth of
another by their possessions. This, of course, has led to an obses-
sion with money. Money can be the lover that we embrace and
refuse to release. Money can rule the fiercest and gentlest of souls.
Some will stop at nothing to accumulate more of it because we assume that money will provide a better lifestyle or more fulfilling
existence.

In the Gospels, we watch Jesus gravitate to people stuck in
the cycle of sin. Tax collectors were always included when Jesus
spoke to people about reforming their lives. The people despised
the tax collector. They knew that they conspired with the Romans.
How else would you be able to run such a shady business in the
public eye? The money collected from the people of Judea fueled
the oppressive Roman regime. The more funds that the tax collector raised, the more he skimmed off the top for himself. It was no
secret that the tax collector stole from others. They didn't hesitate
to intimidate people with the muscle of the Roman army. These
extortionists waited and watched. They looked for the sale of the
prized cow or sheep. They stood at the shore and waited for the

abundant catch of fish. Everything was taxable. As a vulture senses blood, the tax collector could smell a buck from a mile away. The more you made, the more the tax collector sucked you dry.

The people in town knew where the tax collector and his customs post were located. If you didn't go to him, he would come to you. You couldn't hide from the taxman. Levi must have been aware of Jesus before that fateful day. Even with his eyes intently focused on his ledger and his hands caressing every coin, his heart struggled with the truth. Tired of the corruption, conspiracy and greed, Levi longed for a change. The back alley deals and the midnight payoffs made Levi rich, but empty.

He never witnessed anyone like Jesus. The Teacher offered more than the exhilarating sound of the coins clinking in his purse. The call of Levi in the Gospels excludes any small talk or idle chatter between Jesus and the tax collector. Levi immediately accepted the invitation of the Teacher and then hosted a party to celebrate his new life. We know that the tax collector included his notorious associates at the party because of the Pharisees' criticism of the judgment of Jesus to spend time with these sinners. Levi must have contemplated this day for a long time. His mind was made up. He convinced himself that if Jesus asked, he would go with Him. Perhaps, Levi and his friends listened to Jesus preach and initiated their own conversations about the Kingdom.

Jesus searched for those in need of His help. Their sadness could not be hidden. The reason for the tax collector's isolation was apparent to Jesus. Levi's reason for his misery was greed. He was the ultimate capitalist. He capitalized on the sweat and toil of others. The more money they made, the more he filled his pockets. He overturned the rule of life: he used people and loved money.

The intervention of Jesus helped Levi to discover that self-indulgence and greed were poisonous. The higher Levi stacked his coins, the more he experienced isolation. He started to contemplate the many people he had swindled on his way to wealth and fortune. He watched people struggle to find enough money to put food on the table as he lined his pockets with their hard-earned wages.

We sometimes make money at the expense of others. We take advantage of situations to enhance our economic edge. Capital giant Donald Trump said, "You can't be too greedy." But how many people have we hurt in our pursuit of material gain? What will we do in order to get that promotion at work? How much dignity and integrity will we sacrifice to close that business deal? We have all been at the crossroads. One signpost points to modesty and the other to greed. The possibility of extra cash intrigues us. The ability to pay off our bills and stop the borrowing from Peter to pay Paul makes us consider the unthinkable. But how will our actions affect others?

People line up for the possibility of being the apprentice of Donald Trump. They reasonably assume that he has literally a "wealth" of knowledge. A chance to be with this master of the financial deal may propel a person into the world of elegance and prosperity. But Jesus often warned us about worrying about things on this earth rather than matters in heaven. If we were truly wise, we would choose to learn from the Master of real riches. Jesus Christ teaches us all that we need to know about discovering the treasure of eternal happiness and He does not limit Himself to taking on one apprentice at a time.

Like Levi, we must leave the world of materialism behind.

We should not hesitate to join Jesus on a journey that leads us to the Kingdom. Time and time again, we see lives transformed by an invitation. Christ summons everyone to alter his or her lifestyle. Peace of mind will not be found in the accumulation of wealth. Instead, the richness of life can be discovered in our connection to God. Use money and material possessions to enhance your life. Share what you have with those who struggle financially. Ease their burdens. You will experience a wealth beyond your imagination.

Our desire to change can take but a moment. Levi rose from his customs post to begin a new life. Contemplate the change in your life today. Once the tax collector joined Jesus, we hear him called by his new name, Matthew. Assume a new identity in your association with Christ. We, too, may change instantly from a life of greed to one of generosity. Move away from the dependency on material goods and embrace Christ. The Master calls: will you follow?

Graceful Contemplation

1. How do you define yourself? By who you are or what you have?

2. Are my possessions the key to my own self-worth?

3. Is there one material item that I hold onto for dear life? Why? What does it say about me?

4. It is often said that we learn about someone by simply looking at their "credit card or checking" history. Would people recognize me by the way I spend my money?

5. Once a person was asked, over and over again, "What do you do for a living?" The response was, "I am a Christian." Finally, the person knew what the question meant and said, "I pay my bills through working in sales, but I live for Christ." Do you live to work or work to live?

CHAPTER SEVEN

A SHOT IN THE ARM

Thomas, called Didymus, one of the Twelve, was not
with them when Jesus came. So the other disciples said
to him, "We have seen the Lord." But he said to them,
"Unless I see the mark of the nails in his hands and put
my finger into the nail marks and put my hand into his
side, I will not believe." Now a week later his disciples
were again inside and Thomas was with them. Jesus
came, although the doors were locked, and stood in their
midst and said, "Peace be with you." Then he said to
Thomas, "Put your finger here and see my hands, and
bring your hand and put it into my side, and do not be
unbelieving, but believe." Thomas answered and said to
him, "My Lord and my God!" Jesus said to him, "Have
you come to believe because you have seen me? Blessed
are those who have not seen and have believed."

(John 20:25-29)

A small obscure plaque hung over the register during my tenure
as owner of the local deli. The small football award meant the
world to me. Sportscaster and writer Dick Schaap presented the
plaque to me. It served as a memento from the Malverne Varsity
Football team after they captured the league championship. The

season started dismally for the team. They were winless after their first three games. Members of the team frequented the deli each day during lunch. After each loss, they lost more faith in their ability as a team.

I was never one to miss an opportunity to stir the pot. I called the group to the counter to hear a sad tale. I told them about a judge who had a difficult time coming to a decision in a child custody case. The judge, desperate for answers, asked the child which parent he preferred to live with. The child responded, "I don't want to live with my mother because she beats me and I don't want to live with my father because he beats me." The judge looked at both parents with disdain. "I will deal with both of you later," he screamed across the courtroom. "Then whom will you live with?" asked the judge. The little boy hesitated and then answered, "I want to live with the Malverne Mules because they can't beat anyone!" As I chuckled to myself as I finished my story, the guys from the team gasped and walked out of the deli in silence.

Some people are born with confidence. Faith in themselves, the people in their life, and maybe even belief in God come easily. For some, faith comes and goes in waves. Others are eternal pessimists who never see the positive side of the situation or in the people they encounter. We all have skeptics in our lives. These people can spread fear and despair like the plague. No matter how the evidence points to absolute certainty, the naysayer attempts to disprove it. My young friends on the Malverne football team had high hopes entering the season, but a few losses caused doubt to spread like wildfire.

For St. Thomas, the crucifixion of Jesus may have been the point of no return for the disbelieving apostle. Thomas had left everything to follow Jesus. It may have been the one act of faith in his entire life. The Gospels only mention Thomas a few times, but every time he speaks, he is clearly heard. When Jesus is told that His friend Lazarus is near death, the Teacher tended to other matters instead of rushing to the assistance of His friend. When Jesus decided to leave for Bethany, the apostles attempted to dissuade the Master from returning to this region because it had become a dangerous place for them.

When Jesus referred to Lazarus' condition as "sleep," the disciples remained ignorant to the true disposition of the Lord's friend. They insisted that Lazarus would be safe and there was no reason to travel to Bethany. The apostles could not convince Jesus to forego the trip, so they soon relented and prepared to travel to follow the will of the Master. Everyone especially Thomas worried about the wrath of those who plotted against Jesus. But in their hearts, the apostles knew how Jesus felt about His friend Lazarus. The Rabbi would travel to Bethany at all cost. In a plea that combined the fear and sarcasm of Thomas, the apostle cried, "Let us go so that we may die with Him!"

Thomas displayed a certain fidelity to Jesus, but the apostle could not help but believe that the worst was bound to happen. Every group has a devil's advocate, a person who provides an alternative viewpoint to a situation. This type of person urges us to explore every possibility when we plan events and make decisions. The total pessimist is different. They constantly assume the worst-case scenario will occur. Even when the sun shines brightly, they expect the rain to begin at any time.

Pessimism is fertilizer to doubt. It allows disbelief to grow wild until it chokes faith off at its roots. Thomas must have questioned everything. Maybe he was betrayed by a close friend or left disappointed by a family member. We all have reasons for why we question and doubt. Thomas carried these questions with him like a fifty-pound weight strapped to his back. He may not have wanted to be this way, but life has a curious way of shaping us. The apostle assumes the role of the "devil's advocate." Thomas cornered the market on obstinacy.

At the Last Supper, Jesus tried to console His disciples. They worried about how they could carry on without their friend. He comforted them:

> Let not your heart be troubled... I will take you to myself, that where I am, you may also be.

Always ready with a question, Thomas responded, "Lord, we do not know where you are going, how can we know the way?" Sometimes people just refuse to listen. Jesus could have been pointing to a map; it would not have made a difference to Thomas.

When Mary Magdalene told the other disciples that Jesus had risen from the dead, you can imagine the response of Thomas. "You must be mistaken!" He may have scoffed at the woman consumed with joy. Someone like Thomas could mute the hope of the most confident believer. As Easter progressed, you can imagine a concerned apostle sitting in the corner with his arms folded exclaiming, "You people are delusional!"

Thomas is mysteriously missing when Jesus appeared to the disciples after the Resurrection. Where had he gone? Did he start to distance himself from the other followers of Jesus? Perhaps his despair had left him looking for answers in other places. When the others informed Thomas of their miraculous encounter, his anger must have burned away what was left of his faith. Now they had gone too far for Thomas. To answer their outlandish claims, the apostle threw down the gauntlet. Not only did Thomas refuse to listen to their ridiculous stories, now he insisted on touching the wounds of Jesus with his own hands in order to believe. The appearance of Jesus to Thomas must have left him numb. His knees buckled as he hit the ground in adoration. A lifetime of doubt transformed into faith in an instant. Shadows transformed into reality. Many thoughts must have raced through the disciple's mind. "How could I have been wrong all these years? What else have I missed because of my disbelief?"

We all have doubts. Some days we are just like Thomas and refuse to believe. Stop waiting for all the answers. Take the leap of faith and surrender to the unknown. Open your heart to the extraordinary possibilities that a life in Christ provides. Resist shutting down before you have heard the entire story. Illuminate the blind spots with the light of faith. When the wind of disbelief rocks your heart, it becomes difficult to unveil the tranquility that God provides. Once doubt starts, it spreads to every aspect of life. Believing in others begins with believing in you.

We will never be able to understand everything, so it is fruitless to try and figure out the answers to the most difficult questions. Leave room in your life for the unknown. Thomas' desolation ceased once he opened himself to the things beyond his sight. Opening our hearts and not just our eyes will be the only way we can encounter "our Lord and our God."

Just as Jesus greeted Thomas and the apostles, the Lord wishes that our world be filled with peace. A true relationship with Christ requires our fidelity and trust. He makes Himself visible in so many ways, but we refuse to see. We want to witness the miracle that erases our remaining doubts. The story of Thomas illustrates the importance of believing without the piles of evidence. Every sign around us provides the proof we require; yet we still hesitate to believe. Take off the blinders. Make your choice today. Chase away your doubting Thomas within and believe!

Graceful Contemplation

1. Christianity is about seeing. How do you see in the course of your daily life (which is really the foundation of your spiritual life)? Would you characterize yourself more as a believer or a doubter? An optimist or a pessimist?

2. The Sacrament of Baptism initiates us into the life of faith. From that point on, we are invited into a relationship with God "to put out into the deep" and trust. Have I been growing in faith? If so, how? If not, why? What keeps you from having more faith?

3. Faith is often caught and not taught. Do you inspire others to faith?

4. St. Thérèse of Lisieux once wrote, "Trust, nothing but trust." Do others believe in you as a friend, sibling, parent, or child?

Chapter Eight

Alone in the Herd

Now on the occasion of the feast the governor was accustomed to release to the crowd one prisoner whom they wished. And at that time they had a notorious prisoner called Barabbas. So when they had assembled, Pilate said to them, "Which one do you want me to release to you, Barabbas, or Jesus called Messiah?", for he knew that it was out of envy that they had handed him over. While he was still seated on the bench, his wife sent him a message, "Have nothing to do with that righteous man. I suffered much in a dream today because of him." The chief priests and the elders persuaded the crowds to ask for Barabbas but to destroy Jesus. The governor said to them in reply, "Which of the two do you want me to release to you?" They answered, "Barabbas!" Pilate said to them, "Then what shall I do with Jesus called Messiah?" They all said, "Let him be crucified!" But he said, "Why? What evil has he done?" They only shouted the louder, "Let him be crucified!" When Pilate saw that he was not succeeding at all, but that a riot was breaking out instead, he took water and washed his hands in the sight of the crowd, saying, "I am innocent of this man's blood. Look to it yourselves." And the whole people said in reply, "His blood be upon us and upon our children."

Then he released Barabbas to them and, after he had Jesus scourged, he handed him over to be crucified.

(Matthew 27:15-28)

In sports, there is one factor that provides an instant edge: home-field advantage. Teams spend billions of dollars building modern day temples where fans can worship their teams. Frenzied fans pack the stadiums and try to root their teams to victory. In 2009, the New York Mets and Yankees opened their new state-of-the-art facilities. New Yorkers adore baseball. You choose your allegiance at a young age. There are moments when the New York baseball fans allow their emotions to get the best of them. The love that we usually display towards our favorite player turns to absolute anger when he disappoints. Many athletes choose to play in other cities because of the overzealous passion of the New York baseball fans and media.

In 2007, New York Mets first baseman Carlos Delgado had a disappointing year by his usual standards. Delgado hit 24 home runs and batted in 87 runs. Carlos had averaged 38 home runs and 120 RBIs in his previous fourteen major league seasons. He had a reputation as a feared hitter, but this year Delgado could not rise to his usual expectations. Many Met fans quickly turned against Delgado.

As my son, Alex, and I followed the Mets, I always enforced the rule that we never should "boo" our own team. When a player struggled, the fans should attempt to pick a player up when they are down. We forget that the players on the field are real people with real feelings. When things are not going well in our own life, we do not find inspiration from others taunting us. I never understood how berating a struggling athlete would assist them in overcoming a slump. Some unsuspecting fan learned my feeling on this matter during the 2007 season. As he screamed insults at Delgado, I leaned over to him and bellowed, "Enough already, he doesn't need to hear this from his own fans!" The unsuspecting target of my wrath slid back into his seat and tried to hide in his beer!

An angry crowd can sway even the most neutral person. We jump aboard the emotional train of others without much thought. The crowd mentality deprives us of thinking for ourselves. The poison of others taints our attitude, behavior and belief. The Gospels are full of people who had difficulty thinking for themselves. On Good Friday, Jesus met the king of conformity, Pontius Pilate.

The Sanhedrin sought the help of the Roman procurator so they could put Jesus to death. As the trial unfolded, Pilate found the Nazarene guilty of no sin. The Jewish leaders would not relent. They played upon the insecurity of the governor. If Pilate allowed Jesus to go free, the governor could be considered an enemy of Rome because of Jesus' claim of kingship. Pilate realized that convicting this man would form an instant allegiance with these influential religious leaders. Uncertainty and fear must have been apparent in the eyes of Pilate. "Turn the crowd against Jesus and the governor will buckle," they may have insisted as their plot evolved. Pilate's will was weak. The situation in Judea was tenuous at best. He didn't need any more enemies.

Pilate's wife, Claudia, pressured him in the other direction. As her husband sat in judgment of Jesus, she sent a note to him warning that Jesus should be set free. Even though the prophetic words of his wife haunted him, Pilate wished to find the easiest solution. Conformity does not depend on moral standards or integrity. It urges convenience and avoids the bumpy road. For the sake of political allegiance and personal convenience, Pontius Pilate was willing to crucify this innocent man. Perhaps Pilate's inability to think for himself won him this mediocre job on the outskirts of the Roman Empire. Creative thinkers are rewarded for their ingenuity and originality. Pilate would rather follow the crowd and wash his hands of the situation.

How many times have we blindly allowed others to influence us? How often are we willing to give in to the will of another? We sacrifice our principles in order to be accepted by people who might not ordinarily give us any attention. People surrender individuality and personal preference in order to be loved and admired. We hesitate to follow the advice of Ralph Waldo Emerson when he encouraged us to "not follow where the path may lead. Go instead, where there is no path and leave a trail." The untraveled road intimidates us, so we avoid it at all cost. But there are great rewards for those that explore new avenues. J.R.R. Tolkien reminded us that "not all those who wander are lost."

Members of the herd can't see beyond the person they follow. As children, our parents asked if we would follow others as they "jump off the bridge." As adults, we jump into situations without a second thought. We must question our own motives when we choose to be swayed by others. Selfishness takes on many forms. Conformity can rob us from witnessing the truth. Seek the truth and share it with others. Encourage people to be authentic and faithful to righteousness. We do not want to follow the subjective will of others. It creates an unreliable moral compass that will surely get us lost.

At parties and social gatherings, we attempt to obey the general rule of avoiding discussions about religion and politics. Some people have not heard the objective facts from another without an obvious personal bias. Pundits appear daily on television to provide defense for extreme views in areas of religion and politics. Our reaction is to take the alternate radical path. Sometimes we would rather stifle the truth in order to keep the peace. But there is no real consolation when we hide from the reality of the truth. When we rationally approach these subjects with mature discussion, we may not only unveil the truth but enlighten others as well.

Trends are born in the heart of conformity. We witness the branding of names on our clothing, phones, computers and other personal items. People have been willingly transformed into walking advertisements. We purchase items with others in mind, even though we are the one using the product. The label must not only live up to our preference but to the image of others. We constantly underestimate the power of uniqueness. Conformity urges us to safely hide in the shelter of anonymity rather than stand alone.

Pontius Pilate demonstrates that peer pressure does not end even though we have left adolescence behind. Adults play the conformity game better than anyone. Like Pilate, we choose to emulate the wrong subjects. He wanted so badly to please his peers but his blindness obscured his seeing the perfect example of righteousness standing before him. Pilate made the same fatal mistake that Herod made. Instead of using the goodness of Christ for his personal salvation, he used His execution for a boost to his already shaky image.

Christ offers an alternative to conformity. He does encourage us to become part of a larger group, His Church. Many critics who view His Church from the outside criticize its members of blind obedience. But these people fail to recognize that the obedience of faith requires true freedom. When Jesus formed this Church on His truth, He provided us with an objective pattern for living. By seeking membership in this institution of Christ, we are given the chance at eternal union with Him. The Church offers us individual salvation by belonging to something much more powerful than ourselves.

Friedrich Nietzsche explained:

> The individual has always had to struggle to keep from being overwhelmed by the tribe. If you try it, you will be lonely often, and sometimes frightened. But no price is too high to pay for the privilege of owning yourself.

The law of love demands that we not be content with the whims of others. This produces a life of mediocrity. We may stand isolated when we decide to do what is correct. People may refer to us as "radical." When we do what is right, there is no price too high when we keep our ultimate goal in mind. We are called by the Master to constantly evaluate the way we act. Following the crowd impoverishes us from unveiling our potential. Resist the temptation to take the easy road that Pontius Pilate chose. Washing your hands of the situation will not make your decisions vanish. Be your own person.

Graceful Contemplation

1. "An angry crowd can sway the most neutral person." Am I easily influenced to the point of being suffocated by the popular views of others?

2. Jesus never preaches the convenience and comfort of Christianity. Do I choose comfort rather than the challenges of the gospel life? Do I say, "Yes," to being a radical Christian and pay the price for being a person of faith?

3. Have you been inspired by Christians who stand firm for Christ? Who are your role models?

4. We never live in a vacuum. Life is directed to either Christ or to a path of indifference. We must make the choice. Who sets the moral agenda in your family?

CHAPTER NINE

THE GREEN-EYED MONSTER

And while they were eating, he said, "Amen, I say to you, one of you will betray me." Deeply distressed at this, they began to say to him one after another, "Surely it is not I, Lord?" He said in reply, "He who has dipped his hand into the dish with me is the one who will betray me. The Son of Man indeed goes, as it is written of him, but woe to that man by whom the Son of Man is betrayed. It would be better for that man if he had never been born." Then Judas, his betrayer, said in reply, "Surely it is not I, Rabbi?" He answered, "You have said so."

(Matthew 26:21-25)

We have all experienced a tremendous victory or accomplishment. When we share our triumphs with others, some people may not react with our same enthusiasm. We are dismayed by the fact that those who should be as joyous for our success, seem to resent it. The green-eyed monster can rear its head at any time. Others seem to pay more attention to our lives than we do. They quickly point out our mistakes and bring them to light for all to notice. They never hesitate to dwell on our imperfections while ignoring their own faults.

Everyone experiences envy from time to time. We have looked longingly at a neighbor's new car or home renovation and wished the same for ourselves. If these feelings evaporate immediately, then no harm comes from our wishful thinking. But when we enviously covet another's possessions or lifestyle, we can lose sight of our own gifts and talents. Envy has no confidence that I can possess what you possess, or accomplish what you have accomplished. It makes me dwell in the cycle of misery that I create for myself. I can't improve myself because I worry more about what you have and what I do not. Envy eats away at the benevolence and generosity within us. We begin to resent ourselves and long for the things that will never fulfill us. Our society urges us to "keep up with the Joneses." As we focus only on the lives of other people, the world around us collapses and we miss meeting our own goals.

At school, I moderate a choir that performs music at our monthly Masses and seasonal prayer services. The biggest event of the year is Christmas Midnight Mass. The most coveted performance of the night is the solo during the Communion meditation. Each year, we practice with the soloists without the other members of the choir present. They do not hear the soloist until the actual Mass. When the song begins, the singer is only part of the entertainment. While most members of the choir are captivated as I am by the performance, the envy of some is clearly visible. Smiles invert instantly into frowns. The choir members have no idea how miserable they appear. Year after year, it's the same story with different people assuming the role of the jealous diva or divo.

When people speak of Judas Iscariot, it usually leads to a discussion about betrayal and greed. But the fallen disciple can also help us overcome the vice of envy. For most of the Gospels, Judas assumed an obscure position in the ministry of Jesus. When we witness the despicable actions of one of the people closest to the Messiah, we wonder what could have made him betray his friend. Scholars know very little about Judas. His name indicated that he came from Kerioth in Judea. This fact made Judas unique in that the other apostles are thought to have originated from Galilee. The Gospel of John explained that Judas carried the purse, which held the funds for Jesus and the other apostles. His association with money has made him the poster child for greed. He willingly betrayed his friend for pieces of silver. What was his motive? Could it be the love of money alone? We will suppose that jealousy had driven Judas to commit the unthinkable. Did Judas stand in the shadows waiting for greater responsibility than simply counting the change accumulated by the apostles? He may have looked at the inner circle of Jesus and dreamed of the day when he would be privy to the intimate thoughts of the Master.

As Jesus announced that His betrayal was imminent, Peter pushed Jesus to reveal the culprit. The Teacher explained that the one to whom He handed the morsel of bread dipped in wine would be the one who would hand Him over. But even after Jesus obviously identified His traitor, the other disciples seem to say, "Aaah, it's just Judas." Did the apostles look down upon Judas? Judas acted as if he had lost faith in his ability to do anything positive. He had chosen to undermine the greatest thing he had ever experienced.

Everyone loves to take shots at the person at the top of the heap and Judas had his sights set on Jesus. When Jesus and the more visible disciples were thrust into the limelight, Judas perhaps felt more inferior than ever. The malcontent found solace in the conspiracy of the Sanhedrin. They, too, were jealous of the popularity and growing power of Jesus. The sooner that the Pharisees could rid themselves of the nuisance named "Jesus," the quicker they could secure their place within the religious leadership of Israel.

Judas rejected the opportunity for salvation. He scorned the grace of Christ. The Lord handed the apostle salvation, but his self-ishness blinded him. Jesus offered him a place on His throne, but the apostle wanted instant glory. He preferred the attention and the money of the Sanhedrin to the grace of Christ. Envy is deceptive. It makes us look to the unessential instead to what is important. It fuels doubt and accentuates our flaws. We remain stagnant by comparing ourselves to others. We dive into the well of self-pity with no desire to be rescued.

English philosopher, Bertrand Russell stated:

> Envy consists in seeing things never in themselves, but only in their relations. If you desire glory, you may envy Napoleon, but Napoleon envied Caesar, Caesar envied Alexander, and Alexander, I dare say, envied Hercules, who never existed.

Envy is the disease that spreads with the victim's being un-aware that it has overtaken him or her. With our eyes transfixed upon someone else, we cannot overcome this illness until we recog-nize the jealousy that eats away at our very soul.

The first step in the process of overcoming envy is discovering our own talents and strengths. Ask others to help you list the quali-ties that make you extraordinary. Everyone has gifts that make him or her special. If you have not yet discovered them, you have not looked hard enough! Individuality means that each person pos-sesses unique traits that others do not. When we concentrate on others, we overlook our greatest assets.

Count your blessings. Be thankful for the people in your life. As we start to focus on people, material things will seem insignificant. Invest in your relationships. When we incorporate love into the world, we will want the best for everyone we encounter. Envy and resentment will be replaced by generosity. Embrace the joys and triumphs of others. These positive feelings will permeate your own being. Your victories will also be magnified when shared with others.

Set goals for yourself based on your own hopes and dreams. Just because others appear to find enjoyment in their possession of a particular object or participation in some activity, that does not mean that you will experience the same happiness. Never underestimate the old cliché that warns us, "The grass is always greener on the other side of the fence."

Eliminate the thoughts that pollute your soul. When you begin to realize the feelings of envy, change your mindset and take control of your emotions. Put energy into other things. Follow your own passion. There is no tranquility in the sea of envy. Change direction and sail into calmer waters. As with worry, the best way to dispel envy is to move into action. Be authentic and stop trying to copy others. Choose the road that Judas refused to follow and gravitate to a life in Christ. Worry about yourself and your own spiritual well-being. Learn to be happy for others. Share in their joy and witness how the goodness in your life will blossom. Let go of the Judas inside of you and begin to discover a greater sense of yourself.

Graceful Contemplation

1. Resentment, like envy, is the sin that is never satisfied. Reflect on your own challenges in this area. How do you control envy when it gets the best of you?

2. We often do not talk about the Tenth Commandment – "You shall not covet" – yet this is an obstacle to spiritual growth. When this occurs, what personal gifts and talents do I lose sight of at that time?

3. Jesus calls us to be in communion, sharing the successes and failures of others. Do I rejoice with the rejoicing and mourn with the mourning?

4. People unfairly take shots at the person at the top of the heap. This is a reminder that we have been the person that others love to hate and the one who despises another. Give this some thought.

CHAPTER TEN

THE BYSTANDER

As they led him away they took hold of a certain Simon, a Cyrenian, who was coming in from the country; and after laying the cross on him, they made him carry it behind Jesus. *(Luke 23:26)*

In 2009, ABC News featured a new show called *What Would You Do?* The camera crew set up different scenarios to see how people would react. A baby left alone in the car, a woman being harassed by a persistent pursuer and a clerk stealing from a blind customer were all secretly videotaped as people were put to the test. The onlookers responded in a variety of ways. Some jumped immediately into action while others stood by passively as the events unfolded around them. Experiments like this show humanity at its best and at its worst.

It is very easy to look the other way when a difficult situation arises. Noninvolvement costs us absolutely nothing. We conserve our time and energy for more essential tasks. When we look around us, we may assume that we can count on some people more than others. Jesus tried to erase our preconceived notions as He told the parable of the Good Samaritan. He knew how prejudice obscured the way we see other people. He presented a new standard: everyone deserves the same attention whether we love them or not. Love does not discriminate. He explained to His followers that we must search for those in need. We may be called into action at the most inopportune moments.

On the day Jesus died, the crowds assembled to witness the latest Roman spectacle. Morbid curiosity drew people to a crucifixion. Unhealthy voyeuristic tendencies cause us to watch people as they suffer. We can't seem to avert our eyes. Simon could not help but stare at the activity on this day. Business probably brought Simon to Jerusalem from his native Cyrene in North Africa. He watched the crucifixion, as a person would follow their favorite sport. But this day is as much about what Simon saw as his being seen.

The path to Calvary was difficult for Jesus. Pontius Pilate had him scourged to teach a lesson that no one could ever forget. This beating left Jesus too weak to bear the weight of His cross. As Jesus stumbled again, the guards grew impatient. Aware of the inability of Jesus to shoulder his responsibility, the centurion made a snap decision. He plucked a bystander from the crowd. Simon's shoulders appeared able enough to handle what the Nazarene could not. For the guard and the crowd, the crucifixion could resume as scheduled. Simon simply wanted to watch and then be on his way. But when the Roman army called you into service, you responded. They did not care if you had other things to do. For Simon, it would have been far easier to remain on the sidelines on Good Friday.

There are many reasons why we jump into action. Some people are pressured to come to the assistance of others while some do it without a second thought. Benevolence manifests itself in many ways. Sometimes we require a little push to respond. The Gospels reinforce the importance of generosity and Simon demonstrates the need to bear the cross for others.

Because we develop the habit of worrying about ourselves, we have failed to notice when people require our assistance. We assume that the suffering of others will be obvious to us. We wait for the tears to flow as a signal of distress. Many people hide their sorrow well. They manage to bury it deep beneath a carefree smile and a lightsome attitude. Only true communication peels away the layers that reveal our genuine feelings. Take the time to look deeply into the hearts of the people around you. We should never hesitate to invest our time in others.

Simon exhibited a spontaneous selflessness. Real love can be inconvenient. It demands that we act in the moment and not wait until our schedule clears. We must cast aside our own agenda in favor of the wants and needs of someone else. True love costs. It soaks up our time and energy. We cannot be afraid of this cost. The busier we become, the more difficult it is to pause and assist each other. The habit of generosity takes practice.

We can be called at any time to bear the cross of another. Our generosity may require us to be associated with someone who is not at the top of the popularity polls. People may wonder why we would be involved with such a questionable character. We might have to leave another task that was important to us. Assuming the role of an authentic Christian may mean that we would be judged guilty by association. Like love, it is an art, which must become part of us. It provides the strength that can carry any cross. Move off the sidelines and reach out to those people around you who need you. Don't wait until it is convenient for you to act.

Graceful Contemplation

1. What is God's will for you? The person in front of you! Now. Yes, now! How do you react to those who are right before you? Are you a bystander or participant? Are you hesitant to jump in to assist others? What keeps you on the sidelines?

2. People who have great sight often choose blindness. It is easier for me not to see and avoid responsibility rather than to be responsible. What about you? How perceptive is your vision and your response level?

3. I often believe that Jesus came so that we could answer Cain's question – "Am I my brother's keeper?" How have I answered this question lately based on the quality of my life?

CHAPTER ELEVEN

HYPOCRITICAL THINKING

Then Jesus spoke to the crowds and to his disciples, saying, "The scribes and the Pharisees have taken their seat on the chair of Moses. Therefore, do and observe all things whatsoever they tell you, but do not follow their example. For they preach, but they do not practice. They tie up heavy burdens hard to carry and lay them on people's shoulders, but they will not lift a finger to move them. All their works are performed to be seen. They widen their phylacteries and lengthen their tassels. They love places of honor at banquets, seats of honor in synagogues, greetings in marketplaces, and the salutation 'Rabbi.' As for you, do not be called 'Rabbi.' You have but one teacher, and you are all brothers. Call no one on earth your father; you have but one Father in heaven. Do not be called 'Master'; you have but one master, the Messiah. The greatest among you must be your servant. Whoever exalts himself will be humbled; but whoever humbles himself will be exalted. Woe to you, scribes and Pharisees, you hypocrites. You lock the kingdom of heaven before human beings. You do not enter yourselves, nor do you allow entrance to those trying to enter. Woe to you, scribes and Pharisees, you hypocrites."

(Matthew 23:1-15)

When a business is sold, the vendors wonder if the new owner will continue to do business with their company. When I bought the deli in October of 1984, I decided to keep one vendor in particular. Kenny had sold meats to the previous two owners of the store for more than twenty years. He delivered to the deli twice a week and since it was the last stop on his route, he would eat dinner at the deli. Kenny was part of the family. Even the customers knew Kenny from his many years of service to the store.

Kenny always shared his vast knowledge of the deli business with everyone in the store. He genuinely imparted his fatherly wisdom. He urged me to make changes that would improve sales and make my store more attractive to customers. Kenny reassured me that he only had my best interest in mind. If there was one person I trusted, it was Kenny.

In August of 1987, my cook's family invited my sister and me to their home in Bavaria. My parents managed the deli in my absence. When I called from Germany to see how things were going, they sounded worried. Although business was booming, they had difficulty paying Kenny's bill. As I sat thousands of miles away, it didn't make sense. Business had never been better, but profits were down. When I called a second time, my parents told me that they had discovered why money was scarce. They wanted me to enjoy my trip, so they spared me the details over the phone. When I arrived home, my parents revealed that the reason for the shortage of money was Kenny's price gouging. Of course, I was shocked. "It couldn't be, not Kenny!" I said over and over to myself. I could not fathom how the man who shared his many years of advice to help me build my business would ever have his hand in my pocket. After I surveyed the data, I realized that Kenny's plot was not a new one. For two years, he had slowly raised his prices. While I was on vacation, he had decided to push the envelope. Fortunately, he was no longer dealing with a naively blind owner who never questioned his prices or his motives. My parents saw the unhealthy hunger in his eyes.

When I finally confronted Kenny, I explained that it was his hypocrisy that hurt me the most. With one breath, he had wished me prosperity and in the next he wished to take it all away. Kenny opened my eyes to the world. Never again would I enter a situation without wondering if a person was saying one thing and doing another. Kenny made me aware of the hypocrisy in this world.

You can see examples of hypocrisy all around you. When you open your history books, you witness the double life of people like Henry VIII. The great defender of the faith abandoned the Church to justify another marriage in the hope of having a male heir to his throne. John F. Kennedy became president in 1960. He drew the admiration of billions of people as the first Catholic elected to the office and as a solid family man. Years later, we realize that he did not fulfill either role very well. History has proven that it is easier to wear the Christian label than to live the lifestyle that it proclaims. As people try to reach certain goals, they sacrifice important principles.

Jesus waged the battle against hypocrisy. Jesus' presence threatened the members of the religious community. The Pharisees felt that the Rabbi undermined their control and authority over the people. They were jealous that Jesus diverted their attention away from those in control of religious life in Judea. They felt that His willingness to mingle with tax collectors and prostitutes caused Him to be ceremonially unclean. As the animosity of the Pharisees increased for Jesus, so did their hypocritical actions.

The condition of the Pharisees is not unusual. People immersed into the world of religion often forget their true mission and purpose. The Pharisees concentrated on religious practice and knowledge of the law. Unfortunately, many members of the Sanhedrin omitted a personal relationship with God from their lives. Focusing on the rules, they overlooked the reasons why the laws were created. They ignored the author of religion, God. They lost sight of the true purpose of why they were called to worship.

As the Pharisees sought to mount a case against Jesus, their hypocrisy became more evident. They criticized the apostles for gleaning grain from the fields on the Sabbath. In their blind zeal, they disregarded simple human needs. When Jesus dined with sinners, they admonished Him that any person who did not conform to the mold of righteousness should be rejected. As the Pharisees attempted to correct the ways of Jesus, they committed their own sins.

Hypocrisy means that a person will say one thing and do another. We do not have to back up our words with actions. The hypocrites clothe their sin with a false sense of virtue. Outward appearances do not always depict what happens within. We deceive others and even ourselves with the fake veneer that we create. We do not practice what we preach.

We love to justify our own actions while we judge other people. We scrutinize their lives and disregard the inclinations that lead us to sin. We are drawn to the headlines that proclaim the latest scandal where another politician, athlete or celebrity is caught in the web of lies. But how often do we examine our own actions? Do we back up our statements with virtuous living? Jesus never hesitated to "walk the walk." Show others that you mean what you say. Reinforce your rhetoric with honesty and integrity if you desire to show people the way to Christ.

A hypocrite never asks himself the question, "How can I improve my relationship with God and others?" He or she would simply assume that it was fine the way it was. Hypocrisy ends when we cease lying to ourselves. We must determine if we are acting with the welfare of others in mind. People will measure our sincerity by our willingness to act. Be careful to not condemn others for sins that you yourself commit. The process of helping your friends and family discover righteousness will assist you in finding holiness. We can never enter into true communion with others if we live a life of deceit.

The more the Pharisees tried to expose the weakness of Jesus, the more they revealed their own faults. Read the stories and watch how delusion, driven by selfishness, obscured the truth of the salvation. The line that separates Jesus and the Pharisees is obvious. On which side will you stand? If we are not careful, we may drift to the wrong side of the debate. Our agenda or unexpressed emotions may distort our view and our ability to act properly.

Look to Jesus and pray that you will unearth the truth. Seek self-knowledge and ask yourself about the motives behind your actions. Show the world your true self. Follow the example of Jesus and reinforce your words with love. Love pushes us in the direction of God and others while hypocrisy drives a wedge between us. Live out your faith by your actions. Show the world your true self.

Graceful Contemplation

1. My negative experience with Kenny presented me with two choices – to be judgmental and never trust again or to examine my inner self and take an honesty test. What would you do?

2. "Talk is cheap," so the maxim goes. Do you have difficulty backing up your words with your actions?

3. The true individual acts the same way both privately and publicly. Is this true in the area of my faith life or do I lay burdens on others and then live irresponsibly on the side?

4. Holding firm to the teachings of Jesus is a sure sign of an integrated Christian. This means:

   I have a personal relationship with Jesus.

   I know Jesus has given me a mission.

   I must be who I am.

   Are you living according to these statements?

CHAPTER TWELVE

THE UNEXPLAINABLE

When Jesus arrived, he found that Lazarus had already been in the tomb for four days. Now Bethany was near Jerusalem, only about two miles away. And many of the Jews had come to Martha and Mary to comfort them about their brother. When Martha heard that Jesus was coming, she went to meet him; but Mary sat at home. Martha said to Jesus, "Lord, if you had been here, my brother would not have died. But even now I know that whatever you ask of God, God will give you." Jesus said to her, "Your brother will rise." Martha said to him, "I know he will rise, in the resurrection on the last day."

(John 11:14-24)

The feast of San Gennaro takes place in New York City each September. The largest Italian feast in the United States draws more than a million visitors annually. People enjoy sampling a variety of international cuisine. They partake in many of the arcade games and carnival rides. The music, shopping and other entertainment attracts more people to lower Manhattan than the devotion to the Italian saint who lived and died during the reign of the Roman Emperor Diocletian.

In Naples, Italy, the feast of San Gennaro is celebrated in a much different way. Thousands of pilgrims crowd into a Neapolitan cathedral to witness the miracle attributed to the saint. The vial of Gennaro's dried blood changes from a solid mass to liquid during ceremonies that take place on the saint's feast day (September 19) and the first Sunday of May each year. The miracle has occurred since the 14th century.

Miracles awaken the curiosity in people at all different places on the spectrum of faith. Believers find comfort in the supernatural events as they build their case for the existence of God. Skeptics explore the scientific and practical reasons for the strange happenings. The Gospels demonstrate that even firsthand witnesses to miracles did not always experience an epiphany of faith. Sometimes the more we see, the more we question. Jesus performed many miracles that were documented by the four evangelists. He cured people of leprosy, fever, deformity, deafness and blindness. He exorcized demons. He controlled nature with a wave of His hand. But the most amazing miracles of Jesus demonstrated His power over death and sin.

When Jesus heard of the grave sickness of His friend Lazarus, He prepared for His greatest sign yet. The Teacher made no haste in traveling to Bethany to rescue His good friend. When Jesus finally arrived in town, Martha and Mary ran to greet the Master. The frustration and sadness was evident in their plea, "Lord if you had been here, my brother would not have died." They had seen the great things He accomplished. Martha and Mary possessed great faith in Jesus. Curing their brother was not beyond His power. They were unaware of Jesus' plan. Martha and Mary had no idea that everything was under control.

Jesus used the death of Lazarus to teach His disciples that God's plan has no limit. With all of the incredible acts He performed during His ministry, His disciples only saw a glimpse of the infinite power of God. This would be the moment when Jesus demonstrated that the grace He would provide had no boundaries. The game now had new rules and Jesus held all of the pieces.

Jesus had prepared His disciples for His own upcoming Resurrection. Unlike the sisters of Lazarus, we minimize the capability of God. We take the position of most of the apostles. We tend to judge Him by our own standards. We miss the miracles that occur every day. We often forget that miracles are as much a part of God as we are. We also overlook the grace of Christ even though it should be more apparent.

When we put all of our faith in Christ, anything is possible. We sometimes feel that we have God's plan figured out. His ways are mysterious. We must surrender ourselves to His care. The prerequisite for the miracles of Jesus was faith. He invites us to witness His glory. But we must first focus on Jesus and His grace as well as His wondrous signs. His miracles were only the icing on the cake.

The story of Lazarus reminds us that sometimes the situation becomes worse before it can improve. No matter what happens, we should never hesitate to run to Jesus. We should continue to pray and ask the Lord for His intercession in our lives. Many people initially ask God to intercede when a crisis begins. But as circumstances disintegrate, they sever the lifeline to God and decide to go on their own. Jesus wants us to maintain hope, even as despair emerges. Our relationship with Christ gives us the strength to persevere through every difficulty.

After four days, everyone believed that even Jesus was powerless to do anything to change the situation of Lazarus. But God is beyond the constraints of time and space. Only He chooses how the time line is filled. Many times we pray, we hope for immediate results. God's providence may unfold over the course of a lifetime. Grace is the gift that we carry with us for our entire lives. Just as our relationship with God evolves during the many years of our existence, so does His intervention.

Jesus told Martha, "I am the resurrection and the life." Our bond with Christ gives us hope, not just in heaven, but also as we live today. We can be instantly transformed through communion with Jesus. We need not wait until we die to enjoy the realities of heaven. The presence of Jesus will help each of us to continually undergo conversion until we are ready to join Him for eternity.

The story of Lazarus also displays the magnitude of Jesus. Before Jesus raised Lazarus from the dead, everyone heard Martha's great testimony of faith:

> Yes Lord, I have come to believe that you are the Messiah, the Son of God, the one who is coming into the world.

The miracle that followed confirmed His divinity. Those who believed knew that Jesus had complete power over sin and death. As Jesus moved towards the tomb of Lazarus, we see the other nature of Jesus, His humanity. We witness the compassion of the man and of our God. Jesus observed those who were grieving for His friend and also began to weep.

Jesus takes our suffering upon Himself. We do not grieve alone. Our heartache becomes His sorrow. Jesus comes to our aid, but we must show Him our faith. We may look for immediate relief for our agony, but must not despair if the Lord does not rush to our side. He has a plan and a timetable that only He may understand now. Do not abandon hope during moments of difficulty. Pray patiently and diligently. Our worries will ease with His consolation. We should not only seek His presence, but we must also be the presence of Jesus to others when they experience distress. Help people to replace the questioning of God with genuine faith. Remove the obstacles and help them emerge from darkness so that they can be united with Christ.

Graceful Contemplation

1. God is alive and active each day of our lives. He acts through us, with us, in us, and to others, to them, and in others. All we are called to do is to be present in the moment. What are the miracles that you have witnessed in your life?

2. The reality is "Bad Things Happen to Good People" even to God's Son. Even in Jesus' last words from the Cross, He stayed in communion with the Father. Do you actively look for the presence of God when circumstances go awry?

3. Resurrection is the great Christian hope! We shall be changed. We shall be redeemed. Do you often contemplate the wonder and glory of the Resurrection?

4. First hand witnesses to miracles did not always experience an epiphany of faith! Reflect on those ordinary epiphanies of faith that have occurred in your life journey.

CHAPTER THIRTEEN

SISTER ACT

As they continued their journey he entered a village where a woman whose name was Martha welcomed him. She had a sister named Mary who sat beside the Lord at his feet listening to him speak. Martha, burdened with much serving, came to him and said, "Lord, do you not care that my sister has left me by myself to do the serving? Tell her to help me." The Lord said to her in reply, "Martha, Martha, you are anxious and worried about many things. There is need of only one thing. Mary has chosen the better part and it will not be taken from her."

(Luke 10:38-42)

My students are dumbfounded when they learn that I do not have a cell phone. They frantically wonder, "How does your wife contact you in the case of an emergency?" "When she needs me, she calls my office and if she needs me immediately, my secretary can let me know," I respond calmly. I explain my resistance to joining the technological craze. As I expound on my thesis on how communication has deteriorated since the advent of cell phones, most of my students dismiss me as an old man resistant to change!

People love their personal technical devices. A student recently told that she sent an average of a hundred and fifty text messages each day. My students have become so adept at the art of texting that they can type messages with their cell phone in a pocket of the uniform blazer. They communicate their current emotional status or spread the gossip of the day.

The advances in technology have transformed the business world. We can now conference with people from around the world while sitting in the comfort of our homes or at our desk at work. The various types of cell phones have allowed us to be accessible to colleagues and whoever wishes to contact us twenty-four hours a day. With one click of a button we can send a message, advertisement or any kind of correspondence to an infinite amount of people. People in the workforce can accomplish tasks with machinelike efficiency.

We all know people who can't sit still, especially when there is work to be done. Before they can rest, they must tend to the weeds in the garden, the paint that needs touching up, the garage that needs cleaning or the laundry that requires washing. We beg them to come and relax, but it is impossible for them to enjoy themselves until everything else is done. Martha was this kind of person.

Martha and her sister Mary had invited Jesus to their house in Bethany. If you have entertained people in your home, you know the amount of work that goes into preparing for a party. You may even wonder if it's worth the effort. After all of our guests have eaten dinner, the piles of dishes await us in the sink or to be loaded into the dishwasher. Many hands make for lighter work. As Martha stood at the fire putting the final touches on the meal, she must have wondered why Mary had not assumed her usual spot next to her in the kitchen. "If she thinks I am doing this alone, she has another thing coming." Martha possibly muttered to herself. Furious, she entered the other room where she discovered Mary sitting at the feet of the Rabbi. Looking to embarrass her sister into work, she pleaded her case to Jesus: "Lord, do you not care that my sister has left me by myself to do the serving? Tell her to help me!" Martha bypassed her sister and went straight to the top. Surely, Jesus would reprimand her lazy sister and send her straight to the kitchen. Instead, it is Martha who gets reprimanded by Jesus.

When I first heard this passage, I thought that Jesus was too tough on Martha. After all, she was the worker. She stood alone preparing the feast for all of their guests. But the older I get the more I understand the words of the Lord. Martha squandered the chance to listen to the Teacher. She involved herself with trivial matters that could have waited.

Jesus speaks to us through His dear friend Martha. Our society has opened its doors for business twenty-four hours a day. Afraid of missing the opportunity to make a buck, we never take a moment to rest. Like Martha, we wrongly prioritize the items on our to-do list and overlook the importance of stopping everything to spend some well-needed time with our Savior. As Martha scrambled to put her house back in order, she did not contemplate what she needed to straighten out her spiritual life. The King of Kings, the Teacher of all Teachers was preaching in the next room, but she skipped His class to complete the tasks that she felt were more important. How often do we stop everything in order to meditate on our relationship with God? Do we take time out of our crazy schedule to pray and go to Mass? As Sunday has evolved into just another day at work, we have to be diligent in order to make sure that God is not excluded from our busy lives.

The citizens of the 21st century have become proficient in the art of multitasking. We may spend time with people but fail to be truly present to them. We assume that showing up is enough. Being in a room with someone and being present are two totally different things. We have numerous circles of friends and hundreds of contacts in our e-mail and Facebook lists, but how often do we sit and look them in the eye to see how they are really feeling? We hide behind our computer and send faceless messages. Modern technology has taken the "personal" out of interpersonal relating.

In the hectic pace of our lives, Jesus has reserved a place next to Him. He would be honored if we would step away from our usual routine and join Him for just a little while. Jesus wants us to be conscious of the other side of discipleship: the contemplation of Christ. As important as it may be to put faith into action, Jesus reminds us that skipping time for reflection may leave us empty. We need to find a balance between running through life and moving towards Jesus. Many who read Luke's account of the two sisters may identify with one sister more than the other. Christians should mix prayer and devotion with good works and helping others.

Jesus reminded His disciples that we must be concerned with things above instead of becoming mired in the trivial tasks of this world. How are you living your life? Are you more like Martha or like Mary? Do you consciously spend enough time with God? I know I don't. With an evolving list of things to accomplish, I can certainly picture myself in the kitchen like Martha on that day in Bethany. It may be time to walk away from the items that distract you from quality time with our Lord. The dishes, the paperwork and the household projects will still be there when we return. Focusing on Jesus will give everything clarity. Grace is as close as the next room and awaits your response. Who will you be: Martha or Mary?

Graceful Contemplation

1. "We are made in the image and likeness of God." God is Trinitarian. God is relational and so are we. Our modern age calls us to machine-like efficiency, technology, and constant activity. Do I find myself in relationship with God and others or a mere automaton on the move?

2. "Trivial pursuit" often blocks us from moving toward Jesus. What part of your day do you set aside for prayer and contemplation?

3. The Church needs believers who can integrate the best qualities of Martha and Mary. Are my strengths more like Martha or Mary?

4. Think about Sunday – The Lord's Day. Is it a day of prayerful worship or of Sabbath rest? Is it a time for truly being present to family and friends?

5. St. Thomas Aquinas reminded us that "Time is worth as much as God." How do you manage your time?

CHAPTER FOURTEEN

THE WEARY

Then Jesus came with them to a place called Gethsemane, and he said to his disciples, "Sit here while I go over there and pray." He took along Peter and the two sons of Zebedee, and began to feel sorrow and distress. Then he said to them, "My soul is sorrowful even to death. Remain here and keep watch with me." He advanced a little and fell prostrate in prayer, saying, "My Father, if it is possible, let this cup pass from me; yet, not as I will, but as you will." When he returned to his disciples he found them asleep. He said to Peter, "So you could not keep watch with me for one hour? Watch and pray that you may not undergo the test. The spirit is willing, but the flesh is weak." Withdrawing a second time, he prayed again, "My Father, if it is not possible that this cup pass without my drinking it, your will be done!" Then he returned once more and found them asleep, for they could not keep their eyes open. He left them and withdrew again and prayed a third time, saying the same thing again. Then he returned to his disciples and said to them, "Are you still sleeping and taking your rest? Behold, the hour is at hand when the Son of Man is to be handed over to sinners. Get up, let us go. Look, my betrayer is at hand." *(Matthew 26:36-46)*

Those who know me well understand my love of sleep. During the week, I can survive on a few hours of slumber. But once the weekend comes I do not set my alarm clock. I use the weekend to catch up on well-needed rest. Some people become irritable when deprived of sleep. My mind transforms from a well-functioning machine into a bowl of jelly. My response time to questions lengthens. Everything seems cloudy.

Transatlantic flights have always been a challenge for me. I rarely sleep on the plane, so once we land, I begin anticipating checking into my hotel room for a long nap. A few years ago, I arranged a pilgrimage for our school to Ireland. Once we landed at 7:00 a.m., we planned a quick stop at the Cliffs of Moher and then we proceeded to Galway to check into our hotel. Reaching our hotel, I conferred with the other chaperones to see when we would meet after our nap. I was stunned when I was told that there would be no time to rest. The other moderators who were pilgrimage veterans explained that every moment should be utilized to get the most out of our experience. Besides, leaving teenagers idle always leads to trouble.

Bleary eyed, I stood in the hotel lobby hoping that someone would change their mind. My wishing was useless. Supervising a group of forty teenagers demanded that I put my needs aside for the sake of the group. The next week together, as we traveled through Ireland, required much of the same sacrifice. As we observe His ministry, Jesus and His disciples had to endure a grueling schedule, traveling hundreds of miles by foot and by boat. In order to complete their mission, personal agendas had to be put on hold. There was little room for individual weariness.

On the night before Jesus died, He retired to the garden called

Gethsemane. This would be His time to spiritually and emotionally prepare for the difficult day ahead. Jesus would not share a moment like this with just anyone. These disciples knew the true Jesus. He brought His closest friends to the garden. Peter, James and John had witnessed what no one else had. The Transfiguration and the raising of Jairus' daughter defined Jesus in a unique way. There was no coincidence that these men were there for these events. They assumed a special place in the Master's Church and in His heart. When the world is crumbling, there are certain people we want around us. Peter, James and John accompanied Jesus for a purpose: comfort, support and inspiration.

When they entered Gethsemane, Jesus gave them special instructions, "My soul is sorrowful even to death. Remain here and keep watch." These men failed to recognize the pleading in His voice. Weariness can make us deaf to the world. Twice Jesus reprimanded His friends and three times He found them asleep. There were many times when the apostles seemed to ignore the message of Jesus. Exhaustion must have made them dopier than usual! Jesus, desperate for the consolation of an embrace or a reassuring word, received nothing from His friends.

The events leading up to Passover left everyone exhausted. In the quiet and peace of the garden, the apostles couldn't resist the chance to get some rest. In doing so, they neglected their obligation as friends and disciples to come to the aid of Jesus. How often have we closed our eyes to the plight of others? Our lives seem simpler when we shut out someone else's problems. There are people around us at work, in school, on the streets, and in our town who warrant our help. We feel as if we have enough going on in our own lives. We selfishly tend to our own needs, but Jesus demands more from us. In turbulent Gethsemane, Jesus' urging is clear: "Wake up and be with me." This call extends to all of our brothers and sisters in Christ.

We know that it is easier to look in at a situation from the outside. Remaining emotionally neutral allows us to walk away at any time. Peter, James and John experienced one of those "I can't deal with this" moments. But Jesus expected more from His friends. If they paid attention to the words of the Teacher, they would have known that "the hour" had actually arrived. This was "show time," but as the spotlight shone the brightest, they shrunk into the shadows. Jesus would soon demonstrate how to persevere when there was nothing left in the tank.

Many play the denial game. They pretend everything is wonderful even though all signs indicate the contrary. Dealing with our problems may shake us from our regular routines and cause major inconvenience. Facing our difficulties head-on can cause our acquaintances to turn and take notice of the dysfunctional part of our lives. The resolution of our problems is worth the momentary pain of embarrassment. When we ignore our problems, we awaken only to realize that our difficulties have not gone away.

As Christians, we are all urged to awaken to Christ. For some, the process may start with getting out of bed on Sunday to attend Mass. We put our energy into so many other areas that we have nothing left for the One who should mean the most. We pledge our faithfulness to Him, but we fail to follow through. Like Peter, James and John we close our eyes to Jesus at the times that we should be conscious of His every movement. He begs us to be on watch and pray.

Too many people sleepwalk through life reserving their energy for the more exciting moments: the weekend, the party, the vacation. However, living a grace-filled life involves pushing through the weariness – especially, when others need our comfort or simple presence. Don't allow your exhaustion to leave others alone searching for answers. Resist shutting your eyes when trouble surrounds you. Be diligent and watch for Christ.

Graceful Contemplation

1. Many of us construct "personal agendas" which in our estimation can neither be changed nor put on hold. How do you handle unplanned interruptions? Do you close your eyes to the unplanned needs of others? Do you realize that the plight of others comes first? Are you alert to the needs of Christ, even when you are exhausted?

2. "When the world is crumbling, there are certain people we want around us." Jesus had Peter, James, and John. Who are your spiritual companions who comfort, support, and give you inspiration?

3. Physical fatigue and, perhaps more so, psychic exhaustion touch all of us at one time or another. Sometimes we can only rest; other times, we must push forward. How do you push forward in times of weariness?

4. Many often sleepwalk during weekdays of life and only resuscitate on weekends. How can I find meaning each and every day?

5. Did it ever occur to you that we can become overwhelmed by weariness and fatigue, because we do not face our problems?

6. When "we awaken to Christ" through sharing our burdens with others, we find ourselves more at peace and less restless. A wise person once said, "A burden shared is a burden halved." Is this your experience?

CHAPTER FIFTEEN

THE NICK OF TIME

For God so loved the world that he gave his only Son, so that everyone who believes in him might not perish but might have eternal life, for God did not send his Son into the world to condemn the world, but that the world might be saved through him. Whoever believes in him will not be condemned, but whoever does not believe has already been condemned, because he has not believed in the name of the only Son of God. And this is the verdict, that the light came into the world, but people preferred darkness to light, because their works were evil. For everyone who does wicked things hates the light and does not come toward the light, so that his works might not be exposed. But whoever lives the truth comes to the light, so that his works may be clearly seen as done in God. *(John 3:16-21)*

My friend, Frank, recently put an album together of contemporary Christian music that he had written and performed over several years. He worked with a graphic artist to design the cover for his new CD. The finished product featured a guitar against a backdrop of clouds. Upon seeing the cover, I remarked how much I liked it, but wondered if a religious theme could be

more evident. My friend insisted that the clouds which symbol-
ized heaven were central to the design and adequately conveyed a
spiritual message.

As I suggested some alternative design ideas, Frank revealed
his actual motive. When Frank began to spread the word about his
new project, some wondered if he was now "born again." Frank
worried about how people might perceive him. Would they call
him a "holy roller" or worse yet a "Jesus freak"? We have seen the
perception of those types of people: "They live in a dream world,"
"They can't think for themselves," "He or she belongs to some kind
of a cult."

Frank's project became a Christian music album that was
afraid to show its affiliation with Christ. Frank's hesitation to be
linked with Jesus is not an isolated incident. During the 2008
presidential campaign, Mike Huckabee's team produced a Christmas message. As the former Arkansas Governor wished viewers a
"Merry Christmas," a bookcase appeared in the background as the
camera panned through the scene. Critics insisted that Huckabee
had used the cross-shaped bookcase shelves to secretly promote his
association with Christ. Others argued that the politician had used
the bookcase to send a subliminal message that he was too afraid
to reveal up front. Huckabee and his camp argued, "The bookcase
was just a bookcase." People are always suspicious of politicians
and especially those who have an association with Jesus. Whether
Huckabee used the subliminal message of the cross can be debated
forever. Many politicians have downplayed their relationship as a
Christian so as to not "offend" or scare potential voters.

Nicodemus held an influential position in the Sanhedrin. As
a religious leader, he was very much aware of Jesus and His teach-

ings. Jesus and His message intrigued Nicodemus. This member of the Sanhedrin, unlike his colleagues, seemed to actually care about his relationship with God. Nicodemus had questions that only Jesus could answer. But there was a major obstacle that stood between Nicodemus and Jesus: the Sanhedrin. Instead of speaking to Jesus, the other religious leaders spoke about the Teacher behind closed doors. Rather than embracing His message, the Sanhedrin dissected every word. They certainly wouldn't approve of Nicodemus if he went to visit the Teacher.

Nicodemus formulated his plan. He would meet Jesus under the cover of darkness. Their clandestine encounter would take place at night when it was not as easy for the eyes of his colleagues to notice his curiosity. The religious leader longed to elevate his relationship with God. Nicodemus recognized the need for salvation. "Could Jesus be the answer?", the man pondered. Nicodemus was unsure. He must see for himself. So he went and listened to Jesus. The shaky faith of Nicodemus had misunderstood the meaning of the Master's words. The Pharisee thought that Jesus meant that a person had to literally reenter the womb in order to be "born again." In reality, Jesus urged Nicodemus to reshape his life. The ignorance of Nicodemus prevented the lesson of Jesus from taking root. In turn, Jesus questioned the credentials of Nicodemus as a teacher and as a religious leader:

> You are a teacher of Israel and you do not understand this. Amen, amen, I say to you, we speak of what we know and we testify to what we have seen. But you people do not accept our testimony. If I tell you about earthly things and you do not believe, how will you believe if I tell you about heavenly things?   *(John 3:10-12)*

Unfortunately, Nicodemus suffered from the same affliction as many of the other Pharisees. While worrying about the mundane affairs of religion, they forgot about the profound effects that a relationship with the Lord might have on their lives. People permit ordinary distractions to keep them from acknowledging the importance of God. The Pharisees taught religion, but did not live it. Nicodemus had to make a choice. Redemption and salvation were placed before him. How could he pass up this incredible opportunity? Nicodemus had studied religion for most of his life. But Jesus presented something different from the scriptures that he had memorized. In the beauty of all he read, he had never once experienced the grace that Jesus offered. In order to find fulfillment, he must walk with Jesus in the light as well as the darkness.

We often keep a relationship with Jesus a secret. In today's society, those with devotion to Christ are often lumped into the bin of zealous fanatics. So even if we desire a relationship with God, we wait until Sunday to show any outward sign, if any, of our faithfulness. We wonder if others will brand us with the label of "Jesus freak" because of our spiritual affiliation. The Christian rock group, DC Talk posed the question that many ponder in their song "Jesus Freak":

> What will people think when they hear that I'm a Jesus freak. What will people do when they find that it's true. People say that I'm strange, does it make me stranger. But my best friend was born in a manger.

People may raise their eyebrows when they learn of our relationship with Christ. They may whisper. They may point fingers. Their discomfort is only a reflection of their own personal battle with faith. We need not apologize for seeking answers from Jesus, and we should not hesitate to invite them to join us. A friendship with Christ is too valuable to hide in the darkness. They will see that the benefits of being with Christ are impossible to resist. But if we wait to receive the approval of others, we, too, may miss out on something wonderful.

The meeting of Jesus and Nicodemus illustrates that risk can provide endless rewards. If we desire eternal glory, there will be moments when we will face difficult choices. Will we go to Jesus, the Teacher, so that He can enlighten us? We can move from the obscurity of night and stand as a witness to Christ. As the plot mounted against Jesus, Nicodemus defended his new friend. He questioned his colleagues' approach as they rendered their guilty verdict before Jesus had ever reached trial.

Nicodemus eventually made his decision that there could be no more clandestine meetings. The members of the Sanhedrin ridiculed Nicodemus and, suspicious of his motives, asked, "If he too was from Galilee." Nicodemus made his choice, but his colleagues in the Sanhedrin waited for something better to come along. They had their own idea of what the Messiah should be like. Looking beyond Jesus, they missed out on the real thing. No relationship, no grace. It's difficult to see the truth when you dwell in the dark.

Cling to Jesus Christ and illuminate your life. Bear His light and bring truth to your life. Don't allow disbelievers to lure you into their world. Be proud of your relationship and friendship with Jesus. In the moments when people may question your sanity, defend Him at all costs. Study the story of Nicodemus and witness his transformation as Jesus illuminated his life. Seek the light and find truth and grace.

Graceful Contemplation

1. In our culture, there is a false belief that religion is personal and private. When we are in a healthy relationship with others and God, the grace received overflows in community. When this occurs, two things can happen. We share our faith or we make apologies for it. I am either a relational Christian or a reluctant Christian. Which one are you?

2. Part of the vocation of the laity is to defend Christian values in the political and public arena of life. The choice is clear – we can be advocates of the gospel or we can stay in the dark and avoid serious faith questions. Do I embrace the life of challenge or comfort?

CHAPTER SIXTEEN

SHAME AND TRIUMPH

The Samaritan woman said to him, "How can you, a Jew, ask me, a Samaritan woman, for a drink?" (For Jews use nothing in common with Samaritans.) Jesus answered and said to her, "If you knew the gift of God and who is saying to you, 'Give me a drink,' you would have asked him and he would have given you living water." The woman said to him, "Sir, you do not even have a bucket and the cistern is deep; where then can you get this living water? Are you greater than our father Jacob, who gave us this cistern and drank from it himself with his children and his flocks?" Jesus answered and said to her, "Everyone who drinks this water will be thirsty again; but whoever drinks the water I shall give will never thirst; the water I shall give will become in him a spring of water welling up to eternal life." The woman said to him, "Sir, give me this water, so that I may not be thirsty or have to keep coming here to draw water." *(John 4:9-15)*

Meghan stood before the mirror in the bathroom and looked beyond her reflection. The smudged makeup reminded her of the previous night. She tried not to think about the promise she made to herself before she left the house to meet her friends.

Meghan thought this night would be different. She would not allow herself to be used and thrown away by another guy.

Meghan had participated in the "walk of shame" many more times than she would ever admit. She had snuck out of the darkness of her lover's apartment into the bright light of the new dawn. She swore each time that it would be the last. But loneliness and the effects of alcohol have a way of changing the strongest of wills. In the dim light of the bar, he told her how pretty she was and how he loved her smile. Megan didn't focus on his sincerity or his motives. Instead, she craved the attention and the flattery, even if they were lies.

The next day, they called her one by one. Her friends voiced their concern. They warned Meghan of how her destructive behavior would only lead to further misery. Meghan responded with the usual medley of excuses. Her friends knew about her empty promises. They understood that everything changed once Meghan fell under the spell of the next knight in shining armor. Everyone around Meghan realized that her bad habits were hard to break. Many of us have a dark side, the element of our lives that we would rather not mention. It is difficult to break from the cycle of sin. One person whom Jesus met in His ministry who remained stuck in this cycle was the Samaritan woman.

Near the town of Sychar, Jesus sat and rested at Jacob's well to escape the intense heat of the most brutal part of the day. The disciples pushed ahead to the next town to purchase provisions for the group. As the Rabbi relaxed, a Samaritan woman approached the well. She, too, was probably familiar with the "walk of shame." Why was she relegated to drawing water in that part of the day when everyone else hid from the scorching sun? Could it be that this was the only time that a moral outcast could come to the well? Even if she were a woman of good moral standing, no Jew would speak to a Samaritan. These people reminded the Jews of the Assyrian conquest of Samaria. Several hundred years earlier, the Assyrians exiled the inhabitants of the city and transplanted foreigners in their place. In the mind of the Jew, they did not belong in Judea and never would.

The woman had grown accustomed to the stares. She knew that her sheer presence disgusted others. You can imagine her shock when Jesus spoke to her. He had three reasons to ignore her: she was a woman, she was a Samaritan, and she was morally questionable. She tried to convince herself that hostile silence was an ordinary part of life. When Jesus requested a drink from the woman, her life changed immediately.

The Samaritan woman learned to live with the walls that existed between her and others. But Jesus knew that fulfillment and happiness elude us when we build these barriers. In His exhaustion, Jesus encountered someone who was truly weary, weary of hiding from loneliness and shame. Anyone else in the position of the Rabbi would have fled to avoid contact with such a woman. The Teacher not only reached out to her, but also offered her an opportunity for true communion and grace. Jesus recognized the severe thirst of the woman. Physically she needed water from the well; spiritually she longed for the presence of God.

The Teacher spoke about how the water would satisfy her eternally. But it must have felt like an eternity since someone looked her in the eye without the stare of condemnation and prejudice. The command, "Go call your husband and come back here," exposed her woundedness. She was the object of the lustful affection of many men. They used her and discarded her like yesterday's newspaper. But the woman was no innocent victim.

The Samaritan woman was a willing participant in their sexual trysts. The Master's insight into the existence of the Samaritan, led her to believe in Jesus as the Messiah. Because of her great faith, the Lord enlisted the woman as one of the first bearers of the gospel. The woman ran off to the city so quickly that she left her water pot behind. Her experience with Jesus had moved her from a feeling of inadequacy to one of exultation. Once an outcast, she became a harbinger of the good news. Away from the crowds and the high-powered theologians, Jesus made His profound revelation. In one of the most ordinary moments of her life, the woman realized that the man in front of her was the Messiah. No blasting trumpets, no flashing lights, no parade, just the truth. Jesus shows us who He is in the peace and quiet of our hearts. Once we discover Him, He empowers us to do great things. We, too, must bring His message to those who need to hear it.

Like the woman who left the water pot behind, even the things we think are important become nonessential when Jesus becomes a priority in our lives. Our imperfections evolve into something beautiful with the assistance of Christ. He helps us to delve deep within ourselves to uncover the goodness that hides under the layers of sin.

Like the Samaritan woman, we avoid those people who have knowledge of our greatest sins. But no matter how the phone lines may singe with gossip, others have no real understanding of our lives. Jesus does. The King of Compassion awaits our arrival at the well where He will quench our thirst for moral goodness through a relationship with Him. With each act of selfishness, we place another brick between others and ourselves. An existence centered on Christ can eliminate these obstacles no matter how great they may be. We easily fall into deadly habits. Loneliness and desperation lure us into acting shamefully. We may even respond sarcastically like the Samaritan woman when others try to reach out to us. Sometimes conquering our own ignorance can be the greatest obstacle of all. Jesus will treat us with the dignity that we deserve if we are willing to change. Jesus knows that regardless of our past, we are capable of magnificent things. We often ask ourselves, "What does God have planned for me?" When we ponder this, we may minimize the possibilities. We never believe that God would trust us with any major responsibility.

Knowing that our Redeemer lives and stands before us helps us to face the day differently. The revelation of Jesus as the Messiah enabled the Samaritan woman to look others in the eyes for the first time since she had chosen the ways of sin. Not only had she found the One that people have waited for but now she knew firsthand about his love and benevolence. He not only cared about His people, but He cared about the broken, the lost and especially her.

Jesus feels the same about us. The water He provides washes us clean and opens us up to the possibility of eternal life. Cast aside your old habits and join Him by the well. It will alter the way others will see you and enable you to see yourself as you are truly meant to be.

Graceful Contemplation

1. An individual with a healthy spiritual life knows their personal strengths and weaknesses. All of us have a "dark side." Does the awareness of your sins or your "dark side," draw you closer to God and those who can help you in your need?

2. Jesus is the Lord of mercy who offers His assistance to help us grow. Does your faith in God and your relationship with others serve as a springboard from which to begin to change your unhealthy habits?

3. How do you react to the sins and weaknesses of others? Do you become more compassionate or more self-righteous?

4. Are you comfortable like Jesus "at the well" and welcome the lost and lonely into your life?

CHAPTER SEVENTEEN

I CAN SEE CLEARLY NOW

On the first day of the week, Mary of Magdala came to the tomb early in the morning, while it was still dark, and saw the stone removed from the tomb. So she ran and went to Simon Peter and to the other disciple whom Jesus loved, and told them, "They have taken the Lord from the tomb, and we don't know where they put him." So Peter and the other disciple went out and came to the tomb. They both ran, but the other disciple ran faster than Peter and arrived at the tomb first; he bent down and saw the burial cloths there, but did not go in. When Simon Peter arrived after him, he went into the tomb and saw the burial cloths there, and the cloth that had covered his head, not with the burial cloths but rolled up in a separate place. Then the other disciple also went in, the one who had arrived at the tomb first, and he saw and believed. For they did not yet understand the scripture that he had to rise from the dead. Then the disciples returned home. But Mary stayed outside the tomb weeping. And as she wept, she bent over into the tomb and saw two angels in white sitting there, one at the head and one at the feet where the body of Jesus had been. And they said to her, "Woman, why are you weeping?" She said to them, "They have taken my Lord, and I don't know where they laid him." When she had said this, she turned around and saw Jesus there, but did not know it was Jesus. Jesus said to her, "Woman, why are you weeping? Whom are you looking for?" She thought it was the gardener and said to him, "Sir, if you carried him away, tell me where you laid him, and I will take him." Jesus said to her, "Mary!" She turned and said to him in Hebrew, "Rabbouni" which means Teacher. *(John 20:1-16)*

A severe fever thrust young Helen Keller into a world of blindness and deafness. Her disabilities occurred before she became conscious of the world around her. Helen's parents doted over her because of their inability to truly communicate with their child. Helen became self-centered and impossible to live with. Desperate, her parents turned to special needs teacher Annie Sullivan. Annie's objective of opening the mind and heart of an insolent Helen would not be an easy task.

Anyone who has spent many hours attempting to solve out a dilemma or problem and finally experiences an epiphany can relate to how Helen must have felt when she realized the connection between sign language and real objects. Suddenly, life and everyday experiences and objects made sense to Helen. In one instant, the world that Helen was separated from came rushing in.

As she matured, Helen became not only a spokesperson for those with physical disabilities, but also a person admired for her existential philosophy of life. One of Helen Keller's most cited quotes states:

> "When one door of happiness closes, another opens, but often we look so long at the closed door that we do not see the one that has been opened for us."

Helen experienced the human tendency to dwell on disappointment and difficulties. Keller felt the desolation and despair in her darkness. Even after her world opened, I am sure she remembered the days when any hint of hope eluded her.

On the day that Jesus rose from the dead, Mary Magdalene went to the tomb before dawn. Weary from another restless night, the disciple came to anoint the body of her friend. On Good Friday, there was no time to properly prepare the body for burial because Passover was imminent. She would have to wait. When she arrived, Mary was distraught to find the body of Jesus had disappeared. Seeking consolation and answers, Mary ran to the apostles. She confronted the people who knew Jesus best with a strong accusation of his enemies, "They have taken the Lord from the tomb and we do not know where they have put Him!" Startled by the radical developments, Peter and John raced to the garden. Their findings confirmed what Mary had told them. Was this event such a surprise to the head of the Church and the beloved disciple? Did they anticipate the extraordinary, the awesome, and the mysterious? Even John admits in his gospel that he and those closest to the Lord did not understand the predictions of Jesus.

As quickly as Peter and John came, they returned to their place of hiding contemplating what happened to the dead body of their friend. Mary, staring at the empty tomb, pondered the craziness of the situation. It was bad enough that they had killed this righteous man, but now they have taken His body. She bent over the tomb and wept. Through her tears she witnessed two angels sitting where the body of Jesus had been. When they asked why she was crying, Mary once again questioned about the whereabouts of her friend. The One with all the answers stood behind her. When

Mary finally sensed the presence of Jesus, she failed to recognize Him. It was not until the Lord called her by name that she knew that it was the Lord. Mary's despair was changed into joy. Even if Mary's eyes did not reveal the presence of the Lord, the sound of His voice awakened her heart and mind.

There are many obstacles that block our relationship with Jesus. For some it is suffering that keeps them from seeing God, for others it is selfishness. The list of worldly distractions could fill the pages of a book. Many of us are like Mary as we dwell on the negative aspects of life that prevent us from perceiving His beauty. Mary entered the garden expecting to attend to the dead body of a friend. Even though He had predicted the miraculous and profound, she anticipated the ordinary and mundane. As people with a relationship with Jesus Christ, we should look forward to a life full of glorious wonder. A life in Christ should lead us to endless expectation.

Stop limiting yourself. Realize that faith in Jesus means infinite possibilities. Jesus had told Mary and the other disciples that He would be raised on the third day. They underestimated His power. The man that she thought was the gardener, the one who tended to the weeds, was really the Christ, the one who came to remove the sins of humanity. It was only when Jesus spoke her name, that it all made sense. Even in the early light of that Easter morning there could be no mistaking that voice. No person had ever called her by name in such a loving and compassionate way as Jesus had. Jesus came to Mary when she was a sinner and brought her to God. Like a Shepherd, He gathers the members of His flock. It becomes equally important for His flock to recognize the voice of the Shepherd.

Look for Jesus in everyday life. Tune out the distractions that deter you from discovering His Divine presence. The favorite Christian poem, "Footprints in the Sand," serves as a reminder that even though we may not always be aware of Jesus, He walks with us, and carries us when situations arise that require His assistance.

Very often we approach life as a game that is difficult to win. The average person believes that they can go at it without any assistance. When we keep Jesus on the sidelines the hope of winning may quickly vanish. But once Jesus enters the arena, everything changes.

Mary Magdalene had forgotten about the eternal promises of Jesus. We often neglect the positive when we are immersed in a problematic situation. Easter Sunday made all of His disciples reevaluate the proposition of the "kingdom." Now every action, gesture and thought had greater meaning. His resurrection would foreshadow our own eternal glory. When despair begins to grow, contemplate the power of the eternal King. Jesus promises us a reward that is limitless. Remember that each moment of our lives should be enhanced by the hope of our own resurrection and eternal life with God in heaven. When the walls seem to close in, look for the door that leads to happiness. Recognize the presence of Jesus. He wants to console you and lead you to endless joy.

Graceful Contemplation

1. Helen Keller journeyed from self-centeredness to self-giving. She gave the world the lesson that the blind and disabled often have a deeper appreciation of the sensate world. How do you

use your five senses? They are essential in both our human and spiritual relationships.

2. Are the things that block your relationships with others similar to those that prevent you from being in a relationship with Jesus?

3. Mary fails to recognize Jesus. Do you suffer from "spiritual blindness" so that you do not see the obvious manifestations of God around you?

4. Jesus introduces us to a world of infinite possibilities – with promises of joy in eternity. How do you see yourself? Do you use the gifts you have received? If not, you'll lose them.

CHAPTER EIGHTEEN

THE DEVIL MADE ME DO IT

I recently saw a cartoon that featured a man at work. He speaks to the devil on one shoulder and the angel on the other. The office worker poses the question to his two cohorts, "What do you think boys, which way will we go today?" The image of the devil on one shoulder and an angel on the other has been used endless times to depict the battle between good and evil. The angel attempts to persuade the person to stay on the side of moral goodness while the devil tries to tempt him to the inclination of sin. Moral dilemma, complicated by a relativist society, often leaves us searching for clear answers. We question the existence of Satan, a force within the world that tempts us to turn away from God.

Throughout the book, we have considered how the grace of Christ transformed ordinary people through simple encounters. But many individuals have difficulty cultivating a relationship with Jesus because they have unknowingly allowed another force to take root in their lives. They resist grace and gravitate towards another force. The work of Satan is subtle. He is the master of deception. His army is packed with souls who rationalize their actions. Selfishness permits the sinner to remain blind to any guilt or acknowledgment of wrongdoing. Satan tempts every person and, being human, Jesus also battled the "prince of darkness." We should emulate Him in our own fight against evil.

The presence of evil personified remains a mystery to those who read the scriptures. Since his appearance in the Book of Genesis, we have wondered from where Satan originated.

The *Catechism of the Catholic Church* explains the origin of the devil:

> Behind the disobedient choice of our first parents lurks a seductive voice opposed to God… The devil and other demons were indeed created naturally good by God, but they became evil by their own doing. (*CCC* 391)

Because of God's gift of free will, some choose to resist the goodness of the Lord. Even though this angel has been given a place in the heavenly realm by the Father the fallen angel opposed God. Because of his faithlessness, the angel was cast out of heaven. He began to plot against goodness.

As the devil learned of God's plan of salvation, he waited for the moment when the Son of Man would be most vulnerable. The Incarnation emptied Jesus so that our Lord could assume the humility of the human form. This allowed Jesus to live the human experience: to feel the desolation of loneliness, the heartbreak of betrayal and the temptation of sin. Satan hoped to lure Jesus to the dark side. Until this point, Satan was winning the war of good vs. evil. Successfully tempting Jesus to sin would ensure victory.

As Jesus prepared Himself for His ministry, the Holy Spirit led Him into the desert for a period of trial and contemplation. For forty days, Jesus fasted. The devil then knew that there would be a point when He would ache with hunger. When the time was right, he approached Jesus as the smoothest salesman lurks toward an unsuspecting customer with pockets full of cash. The Master of Deception waits until we are weakest to strike, the moments when selfishness provides the only means of escape. Satan tempted Jesus to turn the stones that surrounded Him into the food He so desperately desired. The devil also attempted to seduce Jesus in calling upon the angels of heaven to catch Him if He would throw Himself down from the top of the temple. Finally, Satan promised Jesus endless honor, praise, and power if He would worship the King of Darkness.

Many Christians gloss over this event in the life of Jesus as a necessary rite of passage. We never hesitate to believe that He would pass this test with flying colors. We must not overlook the strength of Jesus in the face of temptation. Every second of His life points us in the direction of how we should live our lives. His temptation became our temptation.

Jesus understood the seduction of material possessions. Satan uses temporal goods as the rope in which we hang ourselves. The more we get, the more we desire until the noose becomes so tight around our necks that we can no longer breathe. Material possessions become so alluring that we buy things even when we don't need them. Attractive packaging baits the most innocent of victims. Look at the faces in the shopping mall. Some people buy what they need and leave, but others get caught in the web. Spending money only temporarily satisfies the empty need within.

Jesus was able to put aside real hunger in order to stay on the side of righteousness. He knew the meal that Satan was willing to serve up would never fulfill His real hunger. How do you appease your cravings? Unfortunately, in the world of instant gratification, we are willing to sacrifice anything as long as we do not have to live without the basic necessities. We partake in the meal that Satan provides without much thought to the danger that lingers long after we consume it.

Satan dangled power in front of Jesus because he was aware of its intoxicating effects on humans. We love to have control over others. We seek the upper hand in every situation. People hate to be subject to the will of their enemies. In order to build ourselves up, we tear others apart through rumor and gossip. We delight as they deteriorate before our very eyes and apathetically step over others as we climb the ladder of success.

Christ stands apart from the crowd, as He is able to resist the temptations of Satan. The scriptural account of Jesus' time in the wilderness emphasizes the need for prayer. The allure of Satan is less potent to the person who is connected to God through prayer. When our hearts lie in the heavenly realm, earthly temptations are powerless. When prayer becomes a personal habit, we discover true communion with God.

The devil hopes to tap the vein of selfness with every temptation. He offers us the anti-grace. Unlike Christ, the devil's offering contains no elements of love. He is not willing to sacrifice himself for our salvation. He wants us to build our happiness around ourselves. Selfishness puts my wants over the needs of others in my life. My unearthly desire for money fosters greed. The yearning to quench my sexual fire breeds lust. The "me first" world produces fertile ground for sin to grow. In his encounter with Jesus, the devil found a man consumed with selfless love. In the absence of a driven ego, sin has no soil to take root. Love conquers all evil. By seeking and being filled with the love of Christ, we will thirst for nothing else. This love fulfills every longing and desire.

Temptation may arise at any moment. We must always be ready to resist the will of the devil. Put yourself in the spiritual mindset before the bait hits the water. Know the options set before you: grace or momentary bliss. One is real; the other is an illusion.

Give your life focus through meditation and prayer. Each year we use Jesus' time in the wilderness as an illustration of the importance of reflection and purification during Lent. A life immersed in Christ can deflect the lure of Satan much more easily than one without His assistance. Satan will try to win you over by showering you with his greatest treasures. His gifts will leave you empty and unfulfilled. Don't be fooled by Satan's smooth sales pitch. He will attempt to sell you on the idea of replacing genuine love with unjust power, undeserving success and superficial beauty. When every act revolves around the love of Christ, the Prince of Evil will move to the next person because he will realize that his work is useless on us. Take control of your life and put Jesus in the driver's seat; He would never steer you in the wrong direction.

Graceful Contemplation

1. The average Christian doesn't rise each morning and think, "How will I do evil today? I can't wait to talk this over with Satan." Rather, we allow our intellect to be seduced and choose to do evil with good intentions for our own selfish lives. What are the evils that seduce you?

2. Jesus is the way, the truth, and the life. How are you like Jesus?

In what ways do you serve as a moral compass to others?

3. Do you surrender to God when temptations arise? How do you with Jesus deal with these ugly demonic confrontations?

4. Do you say, "The devil made me do it" or can you own up and be responsible for the bad choices made along your way?

CHAPTER NINETEEN

ENCOUNTERS AND GRACE

For grace is given not because we have done good works,
but in order that we may be able to do them.

St. Augustine of Hippo

Imagine your family threw a huge birthday party for you. They invite your family and closest friends. The evening is filled with warm conversation and time spent catching up. All of the invited guests came together to celebrate your special day. The gathering is a wonderful outpouring of love. In the corner of the room, there sits a table where the guests have all placed their gifts for you. It would be ridiculous to suggest that the gifts would sit unopened for very long. Even if you waited until the party had ended, the average person would highly anticipate digging in to the treasure trove.

Why is it then that grace remains the present that we do not rush to unwrap? We read the Gospels and still we take grace for granted. We insist that we comprehend the magnificent act of self-sacrifice on behalf of our Savior, but we do not want to fully utilize it. Aquinas and Augustine have explained that grace is the "medicine" that heals the soul so we can be redeemed. Christ referred to

Himself at the ultimate physician. His mission focused on nursing us back to righteousness. Because of sin, Jesus provided grace to change our nature.

Grace changes our hearts so that we are willing to appropriately respond to God. It is a gentle push from our complacent nihilistic world into a life that really matters. God's mercy is not passive. It actively draws us to Him. Do not be surprised when some unexplainable force seems to be pulling you to Him. God has a plan for each of us. The Gospel stories demonstrate that humans can be plucked from oblivion at any moment. Even when we believed that we have been abandoned, God's watchful hand is guiding us.

The life of Jesus highlights the importance of relationships. Isolation has no role in the fulfilled Christian life. Jesus presented the perfect pattern of grace as He constantly reached out to the unloved and abandoned. Jesus insisted we follow His actions "loving the least of our brothers and sisters." Even the most devout Christian has trouble exhibiting care and concern for the individuals who do not deserve it. We put conditions on our love. We reserve our compassion for those in our inner circle. Christ's image of the Good Samaritan demonstrated how brotherly love must be inclusive.

The gentle quality of grace demands that Christians transfer the mercy of God to every individual we meet. The person who pushes his way to the front of the line at the movies, the obnoxious acquaintance who always has to have the last word and the town gossip should become the first recipients of the gift that Christ has bestowed upon us. We may protest, "They do not deserve our love," but we do not deserve the love of the King of Good Friday either.

No matter how much we try, salvation is beyond us. Humanity has flaws that cannot be overcome on our own. A relationship with Jesus Christ provides the only avenue to heaven. Without His guidance, we are lost. As you move forward, meditate on the people who were infused with the grace of Christ in the Gospels. Be aware that grace is pulsing through your veins and mandates your response. You will be called to not only change yourself, but the people around you as well. St. Thomas Aquinas said, "Grace is a certain beginning of glory in us." Experience glory today and embrace His gift. Hop on the road to heavenly happiness. Allow yourself to be caught by grace!

Graceful Contemplation

1. Reflect on the graces received along the way.

2. "No man is an island." Relationship and redemption go hand in hand. What is your experience?

3. Who has helped you be mindful of the power of God in your life?

4. Reflect – review – revitalize your faith by learning from individuals who encountered and were touched by you!

ST PAULS

This book was produced by ST PAULS, the publishing house operated by the Society of St. Paul, an international religious congregation of priests and brothers dedicated to serving the Church through the communications media.

For information regarding this and associated ministries of the Pauline Family of Congregations, write to the Vocation Director, Society of St. Paul, 2187 Victory Blvd., Staten Island, New York 10314-6603. Phone (718) 982-5709; or E-mail:vocation@stpauls.us or check our internet site, www.vocationoffice.org

That the Word of God be everywhere known and loved.